Cognitive Practices

*Human Language and
Human Knowledge*

Rita Nolan

BLACKWELL
Oxford UK & Cambridge USA

Copyright © Rita Nolan 1994

The right of Rita Nolan to be identified as author of this work has been
asserted in accordance with the Copyright, Designs and Patents Act 1988.

First published 1994
Reprinted 1994

Blackwell Publishers
108 Cowley Road
Oxford   OX4 1JF
UK

238 Main Street
Cambridge, Massachusetts 02142
USA

British Library Cataloguing in Publication Data

A CIP catalogue record for this book is available from the British Library.

Library of Congress Cataloging-in-Publication Data

Nolan, Rita.
    Cognitive practices : human language and human knowledge / Rita
Nolan.
    p.   cm.
    Includes bibliographical references and index.
    ISBN 0–631–18973–4. — ISBN 0–631–18974–2 (pbk.)
    1. Language and languages—Philosophy.   2. Psycholinguistics.
3. Language acquisition.   4. Cognition.   I. Title.
P106.N58   1994   93–19418
401'.93—dc20   CIP

Typeset in 11 on 13 pt Sabon
by Graphicraft Typesetters, Hong Kong
Printed in Great Britain by Athenaeum Press Ltd, Newcastle upon Tyne.

This book is printed on acid-free paper

Contents

Preface

Always we speak from the vantage point of some theory, some general beliefs about the world. As if this human condition, *in medias res*, were not burden enough, philosophy adds to its dimensions. The mere effort to raise questions about the character of our general beliefs commits us to more general beliefs: theories explicitly announced and deliberately considered. Thus, thinking about thinking, we find ourselves *in medias theoria*. In light of this conundrum, two popular routes for a philosopher to take are to align oneself explicitly with a going theory and to leave it at that, or to take it from there. In opting for the second course, one accepts without question presuppositions of the theory adopted. One inherits a problem set already defined by the going theory, as well as attendant constraints on the form of one's solutions. Such is the intimacy between theories, presuppositions, questions, and answers. Another familiar route is to urge that inquiry be abandoned altogether, either declaring it impossible or exercising a preference for politics or literature. I do not take any of these routes in this essay.

The problems which the essay engages have been subjects of many theories, none of which I can endorse completely. I adopt instead a strategy of "the innocent eye", avoiding direct encounter with questions defined by debates about: empiricism and rationalism, individualism and anti-individualism, mental content (narrow and wide), realisms and relativisms, objectivisms and subjectivisms, "folk" psychology and "scientific" psychology. My aim has been to approach some of the problems associated with those debates from a direction that might avoid the limiting presuppositions, inherited problem sets, and constraints on solutions imposed by such meta-theories.

But the innocent eye is a fiction, and what follows is meant to have implications for those debates. The problems the essay implicitly engages far outrun those it explicitly addresses. So far do they outrun them that I have had to set an *ad hoc* limit on citing these relations. To all whose projects intersect this one, those whose results differ from the ones arrived at here and those whose results are similar, but whom time and other necessities have prevented me from acknowledging, I apologize for the finitudes. To all whose work has influenced the development of these ideas over several years, I am grateful. A book in which all these were explicitly discussed would be very different from the present one; it would be ponderous, heavy, and denser than this one.

Those who have directly helped me in the construction of this work deserve special thanks. Joseph Margolis and Hilary Putnam gave me sustained encouragement. My colleague, Edward Casey, provided me with extensive and insightful comments on an early draft, as did Susan Haack, Leszek Koczanowicz, Barbara Leclerc, and Howard Rachlin. Their generosity is exceeded only by their tolerance of my departures from their own research programs. Newton Garver, Sue Larson, Mary Mothersill, and Zeno Vendler carefully read the penultimate draft of the entire essay and their comments were valuable in helping me avoid some pitfalls. Thanks to Newton Garver also for seeing the connections in the essay with certain classic metaphysical and epistemological issues, thus reassuring me that my sub-texts were available, even if not transparent.

I was helped by early discussions with: Síle Harrington on language acquisition, Gyula Mago on codes, and Len Rolfe on subjects and predicates. My indebtedness to Gyula Mago is great; both the example of TV and the strategy adopted in chapter 2 for codes are derived from a guest lecture he gave years ago to my class in philosophy of language. Leszek Koczanowicz discussed Mead and Vygotsky with me and provided many citations from their works. Sections of the essay were given in earlier forms as lectures at meetings and colloquia at: Boston University; Cork

University, Cork; Trinity College, Dublin; the Queen's University, Belfast; Linacre College and Wolfson College, Oxford; Uppsala, Sweden; the University of Montreal; Rutgers University; and at Wittgenstein Symposia in Kirchberg, Austria. Large parts of the manuscript were delivered as a lecture series at the University of Wrocław, Poland. Thanks to those who attended these talks for their questions and comments; to official commentators John Bickle, for his encouraging comments, and Peter Gordon, for his trenchant ones; and to Maria Kostyszak for translating the talks in Wrocław. The editors supplied comments from an anonymous referee who persuaded me to work harder at improving some of the weak spots. I also thank Verlag Hölder-Pichler-Tempsky for permission to include content from two essays published in the Proceedings of the Wittgenstein Symposia.

Plans for the book began while I held a Fellowship at Harvard University, for which I am grateful to the Philosophy Department at Harvard and to Harvard University. The State University of New York at Stony Brook granted me a sabbatical year in which the manuscript took final shape; and Wolfson College, Oxford, provided an ideal environment for intensive research during that year.

The prospectus was submitted to the publisher in 1987 and drafts of the first chapters in 1988. Related works on these topics that have appeared in print since then have not caused me to alter my approach substantially. Were I to begin the project now, however, its structure would certainly be influenced by the recent work of Nathan Stemmer (1989).

Although this is a philosophical essay, the fundamental topics with which it is concerned sometimes intersect topics in special disciplines. My interest in these topics is, first and last, philosophical. I have, accordingly, tried to take care not to say anything that conflicts with sound results in any special discipline. I have tried to learn what I could of the empirical work that has bearing on these topics, although no one can hope to assimilate all the research that issues daily from related sciences. Where basic hypotheses in other areas are regarded therein as debatable, I have not hesitated to discuss such issues, insofar as they have philosophical dimensions. If there should be any use for these reflections in other areas, it would not be unwelcome. Throughout the essay, however, its topics are regarded and approached as philosophical ones.

Note on Typographical Conventions

I use single quote marks to indicate reference to a linguistic item. Italics are used where categories, concepts, properties, and propositions are the foremost concern, and where it is significant to distinguish these from linguistic items. Further type-distinctions are left formally unmarked here, for expository simplicity.

Introduction

I

The question "What is it like to be a bat?" captures our imagination: Being a creature whose primary mode of orientation to the world is spatial, and like our hearing; fancy that! In contrast, the question "What is it like to be a human infant?" should be banal for each of us. We were all infants once. Surely, we *know* what it's like.

But we do not. For most of us, our earliest memories are scant fragments from about age three and a half: (1) Mrs Scott, whose house is in a field, tells us to stay away from that plant; it's rhubarb and it's poison; (2) we jump rope, singing "Mabel, Mabel, set the table" and I marvel at their singing a song about Shirley Barr's Aunt Mabel;[1] (3) Irene McLaughlan babysits for us and she reads a bedtime story as we lie in our beds; (4) the people with the strange name who live down the street sell fireworks and Mother tells us that is illegal; we buy sparklers from them; (5) we're moving house and someone is driving us in Aunt Kitty's wooden-sided station wagon; Cousin Joey takes a round, coconut layer-cake out of a box and says, yes, it *is* my birthday.[2]

Freud found more than this; but, search our memories as we may, we do not. Especially, we find no neonatal memories. The earliest ones that come readily to mind seem to be visual memories of events, perhaps under some description, interspersed with proper names of people we knew then, together with some element of utterance. Why have we no neonatal memories? The answer cannot be that the trauma of birth is not memorable!

George Miller's "The Magical Number Seven, Plus or Minus Two" (1969) helped explain part of the puzzle why there is no ready pre-linguistic memory of our pre-linguistic adventures. Syntactic structures enable us to store and retrieve much more than the sensory flux alone permits. Prior to language-learning, such structures are not available to us for use in storage and retrieval. (Ignore, for the moment, the question *what* is stored and retrieved.) Hence, we have no neonatal memories because we have no filing system at that time.

But this seems only part of the story. It is, for example, curious that the early remembered events seem not to be retrieved in the form of linguistic descriptions, even though they have someone else's utterance as a part of them. In fact, not even the remembered utterances (by Mrs Scott, Mother, Cousin Joey) are recalled exactly as specific words uttered; they are recalled only as the contents of utterances. And this, too, is curious. If language provides us with syntactic structures by means of which we can store and retrieve memories, then how come those structures are not recalled in the case of these long-term memories?[3] Perhaps this last is not a problem specifically about our earliest memories after all, since it is characteristic of all our long-term recall. We do not normally recall verbatim discourse nor verbal descriptions of events. We recall the content of discourse, and we recall the events themselves.

However, there is much in the earliest memories recounted above that could not have been recalled prior to learning some language, not because there was no filing system for them but because they could not have been contents of my awareness. My memory includes not understanding what it was to be illegal, except that it was very bad. It includes a feeling of cognitive dissonance at being told that the rhyme was not about Aunt Mabel. It was as if I thought: The song says "Mabel"; the aunt *is* Mabel; the song *must* be about her. But now it begins to seem that none of those memories could have been contents of my awareness prior to learning some language. It begins to seem that language learning contributes to the contents of our immediate awareness. And now the question is, "How, exactly?"

As neonates, we humans are pathetically incompetent relative to many other animals. In a serious sense, we are, like marsupials, not yet done. We are prepared for, literally, *nothing* that will befall us. On the other hand, our comparative ignorance (our under-doneness) subtends our adaptibility in the face of an environment that is unforeseeable before we enter it. For, surely, the less one knows, the less likely is it that one has false beliefs. And it is easier to learn something from the beginning than to extinguish false beliefs. But can it be an advantage to start off knowing nothing at all?

These reflections are preliminary ones. It is questions like these that provoke the main question of this essay.

II

How is human language related to human knowledge such that it endows our species with a cognitive advantage over other species, an advantage, so it seems, in understanding the environments in which our members find themselves? This question is at once both simple and dismayingly complex. To contribute towards a satisfactory answer to it is what has motivated the chapters that follow.

It is the aim of this book (1) to diagnose why this question eludes most current theories of language and knowledge; (2) to propose an alternative approach that permits the question to be asked; and (3) to initiate a direction of inquiry towards a satisfactory answer to it. This is, I say, the aim. But I must admit at the outset that it is a very tall order, and to pursue it requires inquiry at a level of generality from which I would prefer to descend. But I cannot see how this aim could be served by more piecemeal efforts. Undoubtedly, critique of the project will be undertaken piecemeal.

In the diagnosis, three central assumptions of standard theories of language and knowledge are reappraised: (1) that the pre-linguistic child can entertain propositions and, in learning a language, acquires merely the means to express them (cf. Fodor, Barwise and Perry); (2) that the empirical study of language can be pursued independently of epistemic considerations (cf. Chomsky, Fodor); (3) that human language is fundamentally a form of animal communication that is only more complicated, and less ephemeral, than the communication systems of other species (cf. Barwise and Perry, Bennett and Dretske). Central to the diagnosis are an analysis of why a referential semantics for mature linguistic competence cannot sustain an empirically adequate theory of language acquisition and a critique of metaphysical biases that standard theories appear to favor.

An alternative approach is suggested by recent research results in cognitive development and language acquisition, one that also represents qualms and itches as well as rigorously defended doubts about the cogency of the standard theories across a wide range of philosophical literature (for example, Cassirer, Habermas, G. H. Mead, H. Putnam, Wittgenstein). The proposed alternative is that to understand the cognitive interdependence of human language and knowledge we begin by focusing upon these phenomena as clusters of social practices in which one learns to participate rather than as abstract synchronic systems or as manifestations of subtle modifications of central nervous systems – the starting points of the standard theories.

The approach I pursue will give pragmatic considerations theoretical priority over syntactic and semantic ones with the result that theories of the latter are viewed in a new way: as elegant but non-unique representations of certain aspects of discourse and thought that can be relieved of the heavy and sometimes arrogant burden foisted on them of representing Hidden Realities of the mind or of the world.

In effect, I mean to approach the general question above by asking: *How do our discursive practices articulate with our cognitive practices?* This is not a standard question with which to begin an inquiry into the character either of human language or of human knowledge. It is, however, general enough to be a philosophical question rather than one in psychology, linguistics or any of the special sciences. It is also sufficiently vague as not to suggest or demand that a particular methodology that is entrenched in one of the special sciences should be followed in tackling it. Such questions are ripe for philosophers. They present themselves as different from well-formed questions within a special science, in particular by being unconstrained by the shared but often tentative assumptions of a specialized scientific community. Although there are some analogues to such constraints in philosophy – the philosophical Doctrine or School – these are in open tension with its principle of anti-authoritarianism: a philosophical contention may not be supported in argument by a reference to who said it. In philosophy, arguments from authority don't fly. I take seriously the need within each special science for strict constraints on permissible questions, as well as the need for adherence to its body of common assumptions. Such constraints and common assumptions make community inquiry possible, enlarging the possibilities of advancing understanding. But it is because I take them seriously *there* that I do not take them seriously in philosophical inquiry. In philosophy, when such constraints take the form of schools and doctrines they, in effect, limit inquiry and block discovery.

It needs to be emphasized that I am neither endorsing nor rejecting current theories of linguistic semantics nor of linguistic syntax. In opting to consider certain pragmatic issues, I do not mean to imply that this aspect of discourse is, say, more important than other aspects of discourse. Issues in linguistic syntax and semantics are little discussed in the essay because they are not conceived as the main focus of the essay. The pragmatic questions addressed here do not replace questions in linguistic semantics and syntax, where these are understood as components of the formal study of the grammar(s) of human language and languages. Of course, when philosophical claims are alleged to follow from the empirical or formal study of linguistic semantics or syntax, all bets are deemed off.

Because this is a philosophical essay, I have not attempted exhaustive reviews of relevant empirical research. Where such research is cited here, it is largely by way of illustration and example. I have sometimes deliberately avoided discussion of particular texts and authors so as not to suggest that my aim is to arbitrate empirical claims within a special science.

III

The essay proposes to reconsider the general theory of human language, with language acquisition as its major focus. Three questions are central to the considerations I make. One is how conceptual categories can emerge from perceptual categories, and how to understand the difference. Some will construe this as a question concerning the onset, for the child, of linguistic meaning. The second is how logical resources can emerge from logic-free processes (see Macnamara, 1986). This question is not addressed explicitly, although the essay may provide some insight into an answer. And the third is how we might mitigate the difficulties inherent in projecting our conceptions of our own consciousness onto the consciousness of the prelinguistic infant.

It is proposed that very early child speech, where it is descriptive of perceived events, exhibits the extensionality of set theory (perhaps even more constrained to a calculus of individuals). At this stage, descriptive speech can be explained by reference to perceptual categories the child has formed, without reference to general terms, predication, or conceptual categories. These perceptual categories may differ among children, and most are formed with the help of adult utterances of "words for things" and of descriptions of presently perceived situations. The crucial change – the onset of linguistically informed conceptualization – seems to occur with the intrinsic recognition of superordinate and subordinate relations among terms, what may be called "predication". I call this "The Superordination Hypothesis".

If this hypothesis is right, then the preconditions for logical operations are fulfilled with that transition, and non-mysteriously.

Formal differences between pre- and post-superordination might be reflected in differences between extensional, set-theoretic formal semantics and non-extensional formal semantics that are of current interest (see esp. Bealer, 1982; Bealer and Mönnich, 1989).[4]

IV

The issues taken up will also be seen to reflect concerns about the character of consciousness and of "the understanding" in general. It is gratifying to note that there is a congruence, at a certain level of abstraction, between concerns raised in this essay and recent work from the historical perspective of Kantian thought, tempered as well by Wittgenstein (Schwyzer, 1990). The tradition in which the reader might situate my concerns in this essay is one in which Wittgenstein is central, along with William James and the Pragmatists generally. With respect to perceptual matters, it takes more from the approaches of R. L. Gregory and H. von Helmholtz than from J. J. Gibson. And with respect to language, understanding, and cognitive development, my orientation will be seen to have more in common with L. Vygotsky and G. H. Mead than with those who have found inorganic processes and procedures of greater interest.

Mead's thesis of "the social construction of mind" is large and vague by today's standards. I have tried to bring some small and fairly precise considerations to bear on that thesis. In the final chapter, I address somewhat more directly a few broader philosophical ramifications of the preceding chapters. But the essay as a whole is more in the nature of prologomenon than treatise.

V

This is, then, a philosophical essay on human understanding, under the dynamical aspect of the practices that yield, enrich or constitute it. One motive for pursuing an inquiry into human understanding under that aspect is the belief that it will reveal features that do not emerge clearly when understanding is viewed as a state – mental or physical – as an attitude or as an abstract, synchronic structure. In particular, it is hoped that such an inquiry will perspicuously reveal how global conditions can effect local structures in contrast with, but no less rigorously than, approaches to human understanding that are more amenable to models whose basic structures are aggregational and static.

Studies in formal semantics, linguistics, and cognitive psychology have yielded rich representations of many phenomena related to human understanding, albeit representations that sometimes conflict with one another. Yet there are gaps in the picture that they present. Questions remain which the available mechanisms and methods seem not to address, seem unable even to acknowledge. It is hoped, then, that a shift in perspective of the sort that philosophical inquiry sometimes facilitates may eliminate certain conundra that otherwise threaten to become vortices.

Notes

1   Shirley Barr was the little girl who lived next door to me; the song is a children's rhyme which bore no relation to Shirley's Aunt Mabel.
2   If it was "moving day", then it was not, in fact, my birthday, but two months before my fourth birthday. Apparently I thought a round white cake signaled a birthday.
3   Miller's essay drew conclusions only about how syntactic structures enhance short-term memory and perception and not about the sort of long-term memories in these examples.
4   The structures offered by Intensional Category Theory seem not yet to have been exploited for representing intensional structures in natural languages.

1 Language and Cognitive Dynamics

> *We have to recognize that language is a part of conduct. Mind involves, however, a relationship to the characters of things. Those characters are in the things, and while the stimuli call out the response which is in one sense present in the organism, the responses are to things out there. The whole process is not a mental product and you cannot put it inside of the brain.*
>
> G. H. Mead, Mind, Self and Society

1 The Question

What is human language? A universal feature of our species. Perhaps a biological faculty whose adaptive advantages led to its becoming genetically selected for. A category of activities in which humans characteristically engage. A social practice governed by local systems of conventions which confers benefits of such magnitude upon humans who take part in it as to have caused it to become a universal practice among people.

Whether biology or society is most to be applauded for the result, it is a striking fact about human language that it is a universal activity of humans that makes it possible, without guaranteeing it, for our members to cope better with a sometimes hostile environment. In facilitating this advantage, language is thus intimately connected with the relatively superior methods of coping which we attribute to our higher cognitive faculties. How, then, is human language related to human knowledge such that it endows our species with a cognitive advantage over other species, an advantage, so it seems, in understanding the environments in which we find ourselves? How, that is, do our discursive practices articulate with our cognitive practices?

2   Language Realism

One answer, favored since Locke, is that language is essentially a vehicle for the interpersonal exchange of propositional content. It enables humans to share their thoughts by telling one another things, with the result that one individual can benefit from the experiences of others by receiving their propositional reports of those happenings. I shall call this answer "Language Realism". This is the answer implicit in the following remark: "The ability to token and respond appropriately to such noteworthy sentences as 'There is a good water source behind those rocks,' 'There is a freshly killed antelope over here,' and 'There is a sabre-toothed cat just behind you' just when those sentences' respective truth conditions actually obtain is obviously of some assistance to individuals who were by chance genetically disposed to acquire that ability" (Lycan, 1984, p. 240, crediting Dowty, 1979). While this answer is not without merit, the limits that it places on the contribution of language to human cognitive life are considerable. It is one of the aims of this essay to explore some important respects in which this answer does not suffice to the question. But the tip of the iceberg and a shadow of its contours can be sketched now.

Although the ability illustrated in the above quote surely assists most individuals who have it, it is an ability whose complex organization and multi-functionality belie an origin in chance genetic disposition, as if a sudden or single mutation conferred conscious, discursive thought on our evolving precursors, yielding – us.

The evolution of the higher animals and of man, and the awakening of consciousness at a particular level. The picture is something like this: Though the ether is filled with vibrations the world is dark. But one day man opens his seeing eye, and there is light.

What this language primarily describes is a picture. What is to be done with the picture, how it is to be used, is still obscure. Quite clearly, however, it must be explored if we want to understand the sense of what we are saying. But the picture seems to spare us this work: it already points to a particular use. This is how it takes us in. (Wittgenstein, 1953, p. 184)

Wittgenstein is here characterizing, and parodying, a particular conception of human consciousness which we might call "Consciousness Realism". It is a conception which has been criticized by many, including Rorty in *Philosopy and the Mirror of Nature* and Putnam in *Reason, Truth and History*. Lycan's evolutionary picture of the inception of human language closely parallels Wittgenstein's characterization and similarly misleads. The "particular use" to which both pictures "point" is the use of discursive intelligence to represent and communicate truth conditions; that is to say, its propositional use in performing assertoric speech acts and entertaining propositional thoughts. The composite picture that these Realisms present spares us the work of trying to understand how human intelligence is related to the non-linguistic world by simply presupposing an answer to that question.

Consider again the "ability to token and respond appropriately" that is described above. It is by no means obvious that the exercise of *that* ability does afford humans an obvious evolutionary advantage over other species in the circumstances of the immediate life-sustaining activities described above. Members of species less prolix than our own nevertheless have means of communicating that are simpler than human languages but that are, in the circumstances the above scenario asks us to imagine, close to functionally equivalent. A sign of drinking – the inimitable sound of a conspecific slaking a thirst – a food-source signal, the cry of danger, appropriately oriented in space-time relative to sender and receiver, is followed by the correct response of the animal who survives. Indeed, considering only the satisfactions implicit in the examples – hunger, thirst, escape from predation – the greater specificity relative to the appropriate responses that cries, signals, and signs afford may even give them an adaptive edge over our own more abstract linguistic surrogates. Is the water potable? Is the cat alive or dead? Has a territorial rival already claimed possession of the antelope? Such questions as these raised by the linguistic communication have no convincing analogues, nor readily apparent point, in the natural system of cries, signs, signals, and responses that constitute an animal communication system; not to mention such qualms as that the "water" might be XYZ instead of H_2O (that is, imported from a distant earth via satellite station), the cat a domesticated pet, the antelope too high in cholesterol, that linguistic communication can instigate.

Thus are the rewards of greater abstraction that human language affords tempered by the dimensions that may be left unspecified and, so, left indeterminate by the linguistic communication. From an information-theoretic perspective, there is a greater amount of information communicated by an animal's signal just because there are fewer messages capable of being transmitted in their systems, amount of information being inversely proportional to the number of possible messages capable of being transmitted in a system (cf. Dretske, 1981). This application of the notion of information, however, does not fully capture the contrast between animal and linguistic communication, for the contrast is not merely one of degree. Compared to our "There is danger over there" (How serious? Can I finish what I'm doing? . . .), the macaw's scream of fright is, under every aspect that it has within the realm of its effectiveness, not merely of greater determinacy than the comparable utterance but utterly and absolutely determinate.[1] Indeed, signs, signals, and cries have another, if perhaps lesser, advantage in addition to their higher determinateness or greater specificity. When the drinking sounds emanating from one direction occur simultaneously with the danger cry from a different but close source, the latter takes precedence for the survivor, as if both were processed at the same time and a higher value assigned to it. Sentence processing, however, is linear; with some exceptions for utterances of a high degree of salience, two simultaneous utterances will normally merely interfere with processing either. Consider the three sentences in the example above from Lycan, uttered simultaneously, with auditory signals of equal intensity reaching the hearer. Buridan's Ass, one may suppose, was more capable of choice. It is natural to suppose that the exceptions to clogged processing that special salience provides in situations where multiple signals would normally cause cross-interference is an analogue with possible links in natural history to a determinate system of animal communication.

3   Cognitive Dynamics

Although the methods of coping with the environment which language provides do not guarantee anyone or any species a future, one of the ways human language facilitates such coping that is not acknowledged by the Serengeti-plain scenario above is as a means by which a parent generation transmits information about the environment to its progeny, not merely by telling them things but by passing on the language itself. I refer here not to the characteristic of human language that Hockett (1958) called "cultural transmission", but to the fact that such transmission is already infused with cognitive utility. For one cannot learn a language without learning some statements deemed true by its users. One is not learning English if one calls "blue" what English-speakers call "red" or calls "an elephant" what English speakers call "a radio". Thus is the language itself that one learns a practice through which progeny inherit from their forebears some understanding of the world, and not merely a vehicle which, once it is learned, can be used for the interpersonal exchange of propositional content (cf. Wittgenstein, 1953, p. 242, on the necessity for agreement in judgments).

Furthermore, it is not only in the initial acquisition of the substantive categories of a language – what things are called in accordance with the practices of the language community – that human languages reveal a cognitive dimension that is ignored by the favored answer above. To learn what is deemed true by the members of a linguistic community is not to learn much, perhaps, about the extra-linguistic world; but it is something. In particular, it is something to build on. For, with all human languages, the progeny have the option of correcting according to their lights and discoveries the understanding of the world that will be inherited, in turn, by their progeny in the course of their learning the same language. Consider a topical example. Although we hardly noticed it, the newspaper headline

SHE WILL BEAR COUPLE'S BABY

reflected a linguistic change that will alter what subsequent generations will learn by virtue of learning our language. In light of the neo-Darwinian Lockean answer above, one might be inclined to consider that headline as merely another propositional report of a situation made possible by technological change, an instance of the interpersonal exchange of propositional content. In fact, however, that headline reflects syntactic, semantic, and pragmatic changes brought about through the subtle absorption of important new information, indeed the absorption of changes in the world, by the whole fabric of the language. Prior to that technological change, the sentence 'she will bear couple's baby' could be assigned only one semantic interpretation that was grammatical, namely that the female of the couple will bear the baby of the couple. The interpretation of 'she' as anaphoric substitute for a prior term in the discourse referring to some female other than the female of the couple was ruled out by, we may say, semantic selection restrictions on 'couple's baby' combined with syntactic rules governing anaphoric pronouns and coreferentials. But the semantic interpretation that was uniquely grammatical prior to the relevant technological change would also have made the sentence trivial and so in violation of pragmatic constraints upon what can occur as a front-page newspaper headline. The technological change heralded by the headline also has brought about semantic and related syntactic and pragmatic changes in our entire network of kinship terms, certainly in 'mother', some of them already being deliberated in courts of law. It could be argued, moreover, that this type of absorption by the language of a noticed or created change in the world has subtle effects upon wide ranges of terms in the language; to be an electron is, in a way, not to be a mother. Hence, this linguistic change cannot be represented adequately as a mere change in the truth conditions of one sentence or some small number of them.

The example illustrates one way by which languages make possible cognitive feats that have their origins in the social dimensions of language but are not adequately represented as mere communal sharing of acquired propositional knowledge by transmitting true statements to one another. It is in examples like this one that the contrast between the efficiency of signal-sign-cry communication in other species and the cognitive advantage of human languages is most clear. For the former retains its efficiency only so long as the environment remains stable relative to the survival requirements of its participants; exactly that feature which makes it more efficient given a relevantly stable environment – its greater adaptedness to that environment and higher determinateness within it – makes it useless in the face of environmental changes of the crucial sort associated with the extinction of its participants. Borrowing a contrast from Konrad Lorenz, we can say that the adaptedness of animal communication systems contrasts with the adaptability of human languages, their capacity to change as a reflection of relevant changes in the environments of their participants. This adaptability, in turn, confers a greater measure of adaptability upon their practitioners. Throughout, adaptedness contrasts with adaptability on dimensions of both efficiency and determinateness.

4 Society and Language

I have alluded casually above to social aspects of languages. Because there are some deep debates about the social character of language, it is a good idea to be clear that I am not, here, making any claim about what conceptual truths there might be that connect language and the social. For example, in supposing that there are many social aspects of human language, and even that the cognitive adaptive utility of language to humans is in large measure dependent upon certain social facts about language, I am not suggesting that there is some conceptual necessity that languages must be social phenomena, although I leave it open that there might be.[2] Rather, I am accepting certain obvious facts as truths about human languages, facts such as that we pass on our languages to our progeny through social, that is, interpersonal, interchange – rather than, say, genetically, as we do our eye colors, or by writing wills, as we do our material

possessions – and we change our languages, for reasons sometimes relating to improved understanding, sometimes to a changed
world, through such interchange. That humans in fact do these
things is part of my conception of humans; so, in that sense, it
is part of my conception of humans' languages that they are in
fact social in many respects. I do not want to say, however, that
it is for this reason a *conceptual truth* that human languages are
social, partly because when philosophers call something a
"conceptual truth" they mean to contrast it with something like
a factual truth, a contrast that is useful only in specially circumscribed contexts. The present context is not so circumscribed.

5   Desiderata for a Theory of Language

My cat Isis, Jumbo the elephant, and all manner of other animals and conscious organisms have, along with you and me, rich
psychological lives. Of this there is no doubt and an adequate
theory of human language and human understanding should not
suggest otherwise. Nevertheless, human languages are social in-
stitutions that make possible certain characteristically human ways
of understanding the environments in which people find themselves, ways that have so far served to give us certain cognitive
advantages over the members of other species. Accordingly, there
are certain desiderata that a theory of human language should
satisfy. In calling human language cognitively "adaptive", however, it should be noted that I do not intend to imply any answer
to the question whether humans are genetically programmed or
determined to have languages, and certainly not that language
can be *assumed* to be, largely, a biological endowment of humans.[3]

   In the first place, a theory of human language should either
supply, or at least permit, an account of these cognitive advantages that human language confers on our species. One would
expect an account that construes human conceptualization, predication, propositional thought, reference, truth and falsehood as
somehow central to the cognitive practices of our species and as
contributing by the way they work together to the very different
kind of mentality exhibited in human cognitive practices as contrasted with the cognitive repertoires evidenced by the behaviors

of members of other species. So, a theory of human language should be, in this way, *anthropo-centric*; it should sustain an explanation of the cognitive advantages of having a language. But also, in the second place, the cognitive advantage conferred by human language that a theory of human language should accommodate is neutral with respect to any particular metaphysical persuasion. That is, it cannot be supposed that the cognitive adaptive utility of human language lies in its making possible the articulation, entertainment, or believing of any one metaphysical view. Since a rich variety of metaphysical views has been entertained by humans with equivalent fluency and comparable cognitive skills, a theory of human language cannot proscribe the entertainment of alternative, incompatible metaphysical views. So a theory of human language should be *metaphysically innocent* in the sense of not presupposing that one from among many possible metaphysical views is privileged by human language use.[4] Furthermore, the idea that the cognitive utility of language should favor one language group, one cultural group or one ethnic group over another is no less repugnant than the idea that this utility would favor one metaphysics over another. So, in the third place, the account of cognitive utility accommodated by a theory of language should be *culturally and ethnically neutral*, not supposing, for example, that the adaptive cognitive utility of language lies in its making possible twentieth-century physics any more than twentieth-century physicalism. Even if we believe that the development of the physical sciences in the twentieth-century, together with the technologies they have brought, are the quintessential fruit of human cognitive capabilities, the cognitively advantageous features of language must be supposed to have been conferred on all languages ever, anywhere, independently of how near or how far they are to the cognitive products of our own era. These are desiderata of an adequate account of human language.

If there is a theory about that meets them, however, it is hard to find.

Current theories of language can be divided in many ways, partly because the general notion of human language is vast and amorphous, a fact that results in diverse theoretical approaches depending upon the particular aspect of language that is in focus.

Lycan (1986, pp. 267–70) lists seven academic areas (15, counting subdivisions) concerned with the theoretical study of distinct aspects of natural languages. Any easy division of theories of language is, thus, likely to oversimplify. I would like to situate precisely the concerns which I have begun to sketch within the bulk of theories of language developed with some attention to contributing to our knowledge of human understanding; to say that they belong to semantics or to pragmatics or to sociolinguistics, for example. But not all tasks can be simultaneously accomplished and the one of deciding where these questions might best be addressed must here be forsaken. Nevertheless, it is important to note that most theorists of language have not proposed as their foremost goal to produce an account of human language that should sustain an explanation of how human cognitive practices articulate with human discursive practices. Within the special sciences whose domains encompass some dimension of human language (for example, linguistics, psychology, logic) this goal is surely inappropriately general. As a consequence, the desiderata described that are motivated by that goal have not been guiding constraints on theorizing. In philosophy, however, such generality is not only to be tolerated, but is sometimes exactly what is wanted.

It is by no means a major concern of this book to explore various respects in which current theories of human language fail to satisfy these desiderata. Since most such theories were not constructed with a view to answering the question that I have raised here, they should not be faulted for failing to answer it. Having said that, however, it must be acknowledged that I am going to suggest certain ways of conceiving of human language and human knowledge that seem to be at odds with some relatively well-entrenched views of these matters, so the burden falls to me of explaining why the entrenched views are unsatisfactory to one who wants an answer to the questions I raise here.

6   The Standard Theory

I have so far highlighted in a general way some of the broader issues with which the following chapters will be concerned. These issues have been engaged by numerous theorists working in great detail within various and disparate programs and disciplines. So numerous and varied are these that a review of them would leave no room for the positive project that is to follow this introduction. Therefore, and with some reluctance (although not without precedents), I adopt an alternative strategy to represent them, that of constructing a philosophical amalgam that I shall call "The Standard Theory". The Standard Theory answers the question that I have raised in a multi-faceted way that I reduce to four components: Evolutionary, Social, Metaphysical, and Formal. This amalgam represents a broad picture, and some theorists may reject one or another component while still fitting the general description.[5]

6.1   The Evolutionary Component

The Evolutionary Component, illustrated above in the quotation from Lycan and developed extensively by Bennett (1976), von Schilcher and Tennant (1984), and many others, rests generally on the assumption of the Principle of Evolutionary Continuity. This is the assumption that there is no qualitative novelty exhibited in the properties of the extant products of biological evolution. Or so it seems. For the Standard Theory aims to account for human language as fundamentally a form of animal communication that is only more complicated, and less ephemeral, than the communication systems of other species (see also Dretske, 1981; Barwise and Perry, 1983; Pinker and Bloom, 1990). With respect to the adaptive utility of human language, the assumption counsels that it be understood as a result of the greater complexity of human languages over animal communication systems. This greater complexity enables humans to convey to one another much more information than the members of other species are able to communicate to one another. On this view, language is understood as principally and foremost a means of communication of information whose syntactic complexity accounts for its greater communicative power over the communication systems of other species.

Pinker and Bloom (1990) have recently addressed the specific question how the degree of grammatical complexity of human languages could have played a role in human evolutionary history. Their account acknowledges the possibility that more complex speech acts made possible by grammatical complexity could have contributed political, economic, and social benefits for individual reproductive success beyond languages with a "Me-Tarzan-you-Jane level of grammar" (ibid., p. 727). In most other respects, their answer seems to fit the profile of the Standard Theory.[6]

Concerning the role of the mental in the communicative enterprises of members of communicative species, adherents to the Standard Theory are split. At one extreme, we could call them the "mentalfuncts" for their combination of mentalism and functionalism, some hold the view that humans and members of other ambulatory and goal-directed species have, independently of and perhaps prior to mastering their species' preferred communication systems, communication-independent mental lives that incorporate all the same cognitive skills – believing, intending, understanding, and the like (see, for example, Fodor, 1987). I shall discuss this approach specifically and in detail in chapter 2.[7]

At the other extreme are those who would abjure alluding to mental phenomena altogether in accounting for language and cognitive activities. Bennett (1976), for example, offers a Behaviorist analysis of believing in terms of a "record" (registering the occurrence of some phenomenon) being made on an organism under certain conditions, where perceiving is itself understood also as a matter of such a registering. Registration, whether of the merely perceiving sort or of the more complex and constrained believing sort, is something that happens to organisms, human or otherwise, independently of and, in the case of humans, prior to language. Its language-independent character (or, in the case of non-linguistic animals, its communication-independent character) is meant to make registering a suitable precondition for believing and, subsequently in the ontogenesis of language, for the acquisition of language as a medium of communication of the organism's non-linguistic beliefs and intentions. The trouble is that *what* are registered *on* the individual, in perception and in non- and pre-linguistic believings, are supposed to be propositions. The canonical form of a registration event is '*a* registers that *P*'

(Bennett, 1976, pp. 48–59). In the case, then, of both "mental-functs" and "behavfuncts" the cognitive link that provides the evolutionary continuity between humans and other species is the alleged ubiquity of propositional uptake.

The supposition that propositional thought (what was not long ago called "discursive thought") is language-independent and species-neutral is a relative newcomer to philosophical theorizing. This fact has not precluded its widespread acceptance. Nor has the inherent implausibility of thinking that members of species who exhibit no evidence of awareness of such distinctions as those between subjects and predications, entailments and contradictions, assertions and denials, truths and falsehoods nevertheless *have* such awareness. For, surely, if an organism can believe or "register" *that* P, then the organism must be able to believe or "register" that P is true, which must at the least mean that the organism is capable of believing, or "registering", on other occasions, that P is false, that P cannot be both true and false, and perhaps also that if P is true then the denial/negation of P is false. In fact, if "believing that P", in either theory, is to bear the weight of *believing that* P, as apparently it is, then the subjects of such cognitive goings-on must be capable of disbelieving that (for some Q) Q, and, one supposes, of non-believing R, for some R. For what could be the semantic content of "believing that P", if it is not comprehensible in terms of its contrasts with these, or equivalent, alternatives?

It is, however, implausible to suppose that members of other species are capable of the cognitive virtuosity that this evolutionary picture requires, despite the ease with which we project the phenomenologies of our own experiences onto them.[8] Perhaps this ease is itself facilitated by the naturalness with which we assimilate sensing to perceiving and perceiving to judging. For, certainly, sensing requires discrimination among qualia, but we do not have a reliable theory of the differences between, on the one hand, felt qualia (one can think of these as sense data which are not data for anything; "seeing red", for example) and, on the other hand, qualities of objects (when, for example, what is seen is: the red color of a book's jacket). Our notion of perception seems to bridge a gap, for us, between merely sensing something and *judging that* some object has a certain property/quality. But the question where to locate believing and propositional thought on this continuum between sensing and judging, bridged by perceiving, is not easily answered. It is another question to which I shall return.

6.2 The Social Component

Human languages are, as noted, interpersonal. According to the Standard Theory they are primarily vehicles for the interpersonal transmission and exchange of information which operate within a society by means of conventions (see, for example, Lewis, 1969, and Searle, 1969). Within any given society there are standard linguistic practices which must be learned by a newcomer to the society. These practices are governed by rules, principles, and maxims that are followed by the population of that society and that say what sorts of behavior are considered appropriate, sanctioned and the like, by those members. However, since the mere behavioral conventions of a society do not yield knowledge, truth or understanding, the Social Component of the Standard Theory cannot *by itself* contribute any original alethic or epistemic weight to discourse practices. If the social conventions are to contribute to the cognitive adaptive utility of human languages, they must do so by virtue of their relations to language-independent sources of truth and knowledge, in particular, to the cognitive accomplishment of propositional thought, and its attendants, construed as language-independent. Hence if conventionalism, as the Social Component of the Standard Theory, is to permit an account of the cognitive adaptive utility that language affords to humans then it seems to require both the hypothesis of the language-independence of propositional thought (including the assumption that propositional thought is prelinguistic) and the hypothesis that communication of such propositional thoughts is the primary cognitive function of language. But the hypothesis of the language-independence of propositional thought is species-neutral, apparently allowing a full range of cognitive accomplishments to other species as well as to humans (see Fodor, 1987, and Bennett, 1976). The emerging picture of the Standard Theory thus suggests, paradoxically, that in order to account for the cognitive utility to humans of having languages we must permit attribution of the full range of cognitive abilities to other species.

Propositional thought has entered the picture sketched so far as a language-independent component of perception available to any species that is capable of perception. There are, to be sure, important variations among theorists about other aspects of perception, including the precise natures of the relation between sensing and perceiving and of the contribution of the organism to this cognitive hierarchy (see Fodor, 1975, 1983, for a top-down account, and Harnad, 1987a and b, for a bottom-up account). But, independently of such variations, it is upon its propositionally laden and language-independent notion of perception that the Standard Theory founds its treatment of such cognitively important matters as truth and falsehood together with their attendant propositional attitudes – believing, knowing and the like (see also Dretske, 1969).

6.3   The Metaphysical Component

Enter here the third component of the Standard Theory, the Metaphysical Component of Realism, in particular, the realist theory of perception that underlies the doctrine of Language Realism. The metaphysical thesis is simple, and appealing: In perception, propositionally construed, an organism is provided with true beliefs about the world (see, for other examples, Barwise and Perry, 1983, ch. 1, and Miller and Johnson-Laird, 1976). For humans, learning the conventional language of their linguistic community amounts to solving the problem either of translating these ready-made beliefs into the appropriate sentences of the speech community (for example, for Fodor, 1975, and also Miller and Johnson-Laird, 1976; perhaps for Dretske, 1981, and Barwise and Perry, 1983) or of learning the correct correlations/translations of their in-place perceptual categories with the words of the target language (for example, for Bennett, 1976; Macnamara, 1982, 1986; Harnad, 1987a and b; Markman, 1989). The metaphysical thesis of the Standard Theory, working together with its evolutionary and social components, thus yields the conclusion that the language of the community is entirely external and peripheral to an individual's cognitive accomplishments.

6.4   The Formal Component

The final component of the Standard Theory that I shall mention here is its Formal Model. The evolutionary, social, and metaphysical components together coalesce in what has been called a "referential semantics", an account of the meaning or significance of linguistic units exclusively in terms of what those units refer to: individuals, states of affairs, situations, possible worlds, propositions, relations, properties, and items in a language of thought are some of the candidates that have been proposed. The mathematical source of the formal model used by the Standard Theory to represent its referential semantics is set theory; logically, its preferred form is first-order logic. The Standard Theory has as a very strong part of its motivation the goal of generating a description of linguistic phenomena that can be represented set-theoretically and using only the formal apparatus of first-order logic.[9] The reasons for adopting these constraints have often been philosophically deep ones that extend far beyond the particular questions that this essay addresses. Direct discussion of these reasons will be avoided here, since the issues that form the focus of this essay are themselves sufficiently baroque to present challenges enough. It will be argued, however, that the formal model has been so important in shaping the structure of the Standard Theory and in determining its details that many of the shortcomings of the theory reflect inadequacies of this model. In chapter 2, some crucial respects in which this model is inadequate for a general theory of human language will be shown. In order to appreciate the role of that critique in the general plan of this essay, some summary remarks may be helpful now.

7   Foci for Revision

The philosophical, logical, and empirical issues raised by the question asked and the Standard Theory are prodigious; they extend far beyond the limits of one book. The topics that will be discussed in subsequent chapters are therefore selected rather as foci for revision than as exhaustive foundational critiques of the Standard Theory. In fact, I shall argue that the Standard Theory has an important although highly circumscribed role in understanding the cognitive practices associated with human language; but it is not the role that it has thus far assumed, that is, the role of a general meta-theory of human language.

These foci for revision are three: (1) language acquisition; (2) the social component of natural language as a cognitive and species-universal practice; and (3) the role and structures of formal models of natural language. The key to the critique of the Standard Theory that I shall undertake is the inadequacy of its account of language acquisition.

Notes

1   I am concerned at this early stage only to note some of the most obvious, non-technical disanalogies between animal communication in the wild and human linguistic communication that challenge Language Realism. G. H. Mead and L. S. Vygotsky are among earlier theorists who developed alternatives to that view and suggested more complex contrasts between animal communication and human language. See, for example, Vygotsky, 1978, p. 26; and Mead, 1981, pp. 213–14.
2   McGinn (1984) discusses Wittgenstein's intimations about the social character of language as if they raised the question whether it is a "conceptual truth" that human languages are social phenomena. McGinn was I think mistaken in this construal of Wittgenstein's concerns, although his later work (McGinn, 1989) displays, if I understand him rightly, an adjusted view.
3   For a different view, see Millikan (1984). For other discussions of this topic, see Brandon (1985) and Smillie (1985).
4   I do not mean by this desideratum to rule out the possibility that a fully adequate theory of language *might* have metaphysical entailments, but only that the cognitive adaptive utility of language cannot be supposed to be conferred only upon humans who have accepted some privileged metaphysics. Alternative metaphysical views must be permitted in this sense. Hence, I have called this desideratum "metaphysical innocence" rather than "metaphysical neutrality" to

allow the possibility of there being some metaphysics that is entailed by all human language use.

5   What is described does not function as a person made of straw, however. My purpose in subsequent chapters is to show that each component is a defective representation and not to undermine its structure by removing individual straws. Finer distinctions among the many theorists who conform to the characterization are not relevant here.

6   The ambiguity of Chomsky's position concerning language evolution is evident in the discussion accompanying Pinker and Bloom's paper. An evolutionary account is problematic for nativist arguments because Evolution is a dumb inductionist. Either the specific form of the presumed universal grammar has no evolutionary advantage or humans themselves could empirically discover it and its advantage. Humans can be dumb inductionists too; but Evolution cannot know *a priori* rules.

7   What is meant by the term *functionalism* varies. Contrast Blackman's (1991) use of the term to characterize Skinner's work with Block's (1980) discussion of the correct definition of the term.

8   Some do not agree with my judgment of plausibility here, of course, and a consideration of various alternative approaches to this issue would include: (1) the view that there is a large element of decision involved in answering the question whether non-human animals have beliefs; and (2) discussion of a number of complex issues concerning the character of our theoretical and everyday representations of the contents of consciousness. Two important discussions of some of these issues are undertaken by Barcan Marcus (1990) and Palmer (1978). I hope it will be clear, if not now, then later, that I am not advocating a view that beliefs are sentences in a language.

9   For the reader unfamiliar with these technical terms, the relevant aspects of these enterprises will be explained in subsequent chapters.

2 The Code Metaphor for Languages

The interpretation given to the first words of the child is the touchstone of every theory of child speech; it is the focal point at which all the major trends in modern speech theories meet and cross. One might say without exaggeration that the whole structure of a theory is determined by the translation of the first words of the child.

Vygotsky, Thought and Language

What happens when a child learns a language? Many things: subtle and deep and still mysterious neurobiological changes take place within the organism; a special type of mentality emerges; rationality dawns. In particular, the child enters a social institution which confers cognitive benefits upon its members. The question, then, what happens when a child learns a language, can be approached from different perspectives depending upon which of these features is the focus of one's interest. Although there is unanimity that a language is a social institution that confers cognitive benefits upon its members, this feature has seldom been the guiding focus of inquiry into language acquisition. The predominant focus, perhaps since Locke proposed the first mechanical account of human mentality, has instead been on hypothesizing the internal structures that an individual must be supposed to have in order to speak and understand a language. The proliferation of potential models for these structures generated by galloping technology has heightened the search. Certainly there are such structures, speaking is not magic, and the question what those structures might be is genuine. But these are not the only considerations that have prompted so many merely to nod in acknowledgement that a language is a conventional social institution and leave it at that. Another dominant consideration has been the assumption that the cognitive utility of its social character is both simple and obvious: it thereby enables one to learn truths from others and to express to others truths that they would otherwise not know; in this way, the social features of language enable us to learn vastly more about the world than we could ever do by our isolated and slow selves. Apart from imposing the requirement that the internal structures, mental or otherwise, that account for language in the individual must accommodate truths and beliefs, the social-institutional features of languages are thus supposed not to reveal anything that is particularly relevant to understanding those structures or their manifestations.

What happens when a child learns a language? Here is one account: The child has a rich store of conceptual apparatus with which to meet the challenge. The store consists in knowledge of the universal syntax of human languages and of all their possible instantiations in particular languages; it includes also an innate language of thought containing counterparts of all possible semantic units to be learned, as well as an endowment of mental operations and states embracing propositional attitudes – beliefs, desires, knowledge – and metalinguistic concepts and relations – truth, reference, object, property. What happens in language acquisition is that the child learns, by employing mechanical or computational procedures, to encode sentences (propositional formulae) of a language of thought in the language to be learned (Fodor, 1975, 1981, 1983; Macnamara, 1982).[1] Despite its lavish use of the notion of innate mental apparatus antithetical to the way Locke conceived his project of placing the mind firmly within the Newtonian mechanical universe of physical objects whose fundamental laws governed colliding particles, this account shares Locke's conception of language and language learning, differing from his mainly in trading our notion of a mechanical procedure for his conception of a mechanical process. In particular, it shares Locke's minimalist assessment of the cognitive adaptive utility of human languages, that is, that they benefit us by permitting us to communicate our ideas to others. But this account seems to run headlong into generations of enlightened critique of the fundamental picture that it invokes, that of a language learned as a code on something else. The problems with this fundamental picture that has persisted throughout the history of natural language semantics are thrown into sharper relief by the new metaphor in which it has been cast, the code metaphor. For this reason, as well as to provide background for a different answer to the leading question, I shall risk charges of *déjà vu* and ask the reader to consider with me some highlights from the history of referential semantics, framed by the metaphor in current favor. Before this undertaking, however, the question what is attributed to languages in saying that they are codes needs to be considered.

8 The Semantic Content of the Code Metaphor

In 1960, Roman Jakobson addressed the American Mathematical Society, "The interlocutors belonging to one given speech community may be defined," he said, "as actual users of one and the same language code. . . . A common code is their communication tool, which actually underlies and makes possible the exchange of messages" (Jakobson, 1961, p. 247). Since then it has become almost commonplace to talk of understanding and speaking a language in terms of encoding, transmitting and decoding messages. The literature that invokes this metaphor, however, is very quiet about what properties are being ascribed to human languages in saying that they are codes. Perhaps there are some respects in which the metaphor is apt; but we should expect at least that what is true of all metaphors is also true of this one: that there are other respects in which the metaphor is not apt. Richard may have had a heart like a lion's but he surely did not have the strength of one; New York may be large and dense like a big apple but it is not homogeneous through and through. In order to evaluate a metaphor one needs to know as exactly as possible what features or properties it attributes to the new subject.

In attempting to unpack the metaphor and to say what features are being attributed to human languages when it is said that they are codes, it will not help to consult abstract coding theory (see, for example, Hartnett, 1974). For that branch of applied mathematics attempts to formalize some intuitive concept of a code and to refine it for special practical purposes; its definitions are selected with a view to those special purposes.[2] And those who have said that human languages are codes do not, for the most part, invoke abstract coding theory in support of the claim. It is our intuitive conception of codes that is appealed to by the metaphor, but that conception is not spelled out. I want here to make it explicit.

In his address to the mathematicians, Jakobson quoted Colin Cherry that a code is "an agreed transformation – usually one-to-one and reversible – by which one set of informational units is converted into another set" (Cherry, 1957, p. 7), and if we look to common examples of codes, this characterization is borne out. I want now to consider two codes that are used in ways analogous to the way in which human languages would have to be used if they were codes. The purpose of considering these codes closely is to reveal the fundamental properties that are attributed to natural languages in calling them codes – to reveal the semantic content of the predicate 'is a code'. This needs to be done in order to assess the metaphor.

Codes are used for various purposes: shops use color codes on tags for sizes; black-and-white television pictures are transmitted by a mathematical coding of the picture; the enemy codes its messages to its agents. Consider the television example. Although a black-and-white TV picture looks like a continuous image, it is actually formed on a grid containing many lines, each with different gradations of light and dark. The picture that one sees was transmitted by being first represented mathematically; the mathematical representation codes the picture by representing, for each line of the grid, the gradations of light and dark that will reproduce the picture. The receiver decodes this mathematical representation by means of an electron gun which rapidly fires electrons in a row for each line of the grid and in accordance with directions inherent in the mathematical representation. In this code, the TV picture on the screen is the message. If we count as one message in this code one array-type of illuminated points on the

TV screen then there is only a definite number of messages that can be transmitted in this system. The destination, the TV screen, places both a lower and an upper bound on the number of different array-types that are possible. Although the number of possible pictures for any black-and-white television screen is very large, it is a definite number.

Another feature of the TV code that is important in the context of this inquiry is that there is no distinction between a well-formed message and an ill-formed one that can be made purely in terms of the mathematical representation. Any mathematical representation that is possible within that upper and lower bound could represent (an instant of) some picture whose transmission was intended and successful. But if this is so, then there are no structural rules that can be defined only over mathematical representations and that would rule out some as ill-formed. This is not to say that all TV pictures are well formed, but only that a picture's ill-formedness cannot be attributed to there having been some ill-formed mathematical representation. A picture's ill-formedness may be attributed to faulty camera work, to mechanical malfunction or to directorial blunder, but not to something faulty in the sequence of numbers itself that was transmitted. That is, the code has no syntax.

The encoding and decoding operations are matching operations. The mathematical representation is composed of units – numbers – which stand in one-to-one correlation with units of the picture; the units of the picture, in turn, are points on the screen, each of a certain degree of lightness or darkness. To perform the matching operations of encoding and decoding respectively, it is necessary to be able to identify the units of the picture without consulting the code and to be able to identify the units of the code without consulting the units of the picture. Exactly what this amounts to and why it is necessary will, I hope, become clearer with a second example to be considered in a moment. Within this code system, of course, the identifying and matching operations are performed mechanically. I shall call this coding system "TV".

Transmission of television pictures is remote from human languages. A move closer to them can be made if we consider the letter code that Peter Wimsey breaks in the Dorothy Sayers's mystery *Have His Carcase*. The code is worked on a grid of 25 squares in five rows and five columns. There is a key-word known to the sender and intended receiver, and the letters of this key-word are entered, by encoder and decoder, and from left to right, in the first boxes of the grid, thus:

M	O	N	A	R
C	H	Y		

The remaining boxes are filled by the letters of the alphabet in order but omitting those letters that already appear in the key-word and treating 'I' and 'J', archaic fashion, as one:

M	O	N	A	R
C	H	Y	B	D
E	F	G	IJ	K
L	P	Q	S	T
U	V	W	X	Z

To encode a text, first divide the words, from left to right, into ordered pairs of letters; if by doing so tokens of the same letter would occur as both members of a pair, insert an 'X' after the first occurrence of the letter to prevent it. In Sayers's example, the text to be encoded begins "To his Serene Highness...."; it is divided:

TO HI SX SE RE NE HI GH NE SX S...

Then, for each pair of letters, locate its members on the grid. If they come at the corners of a rectangle, as do 'T' and 'O', encode them with the letters at the other two corners, substituting for each letter to be encoded the one in the same row as that one. So TO is encoded PR and HI is encoded BF. If the members of a pair are both in the same column on the grid, encode them with the letters next below each. So SX becomes XA, and for the rest, we end up with:

SE   is encoded LI
RE   is encoded MK
NE   is encoded MG
HI   is encoded BF
GH   is encoded FY
NE   is encoded MG
SX   is encoded XA

Another rule of this code that is not operative in our sample text is that if both members of a pair to be encoded are in the same row on the grid, they are encoded by the letters immediately to the right of each one. This is, in essence, the code. For additional security, the pairs of code letters may be grouped in any way that will conceal the fact that the relevant grouping is by pairs, and punctuation may be inserted at random to confuse the enemy. Thus, the coded message in the novel begins:

PRBFX ALI MKMG BFFY,

The decoder segments the coded message into pairs of letters, deletes punctuation, constructs the grid, and reverses the encoding process to arrive at the "clean" text. Following Wimsey, I shall call this code system "Diagonal".

How does Diagonal compare with TV with respect to the features mentioned? First, if we count as one message in this code one coded text that is, in its "clean" (that is, uncoded) form, meaningful in some language, then one respect in which Diagonal differs from TV is that there is no definite number of messages that can be transmitted in Diagonal, since there is no definite number of sentences in any living language. For such languages, the number of sentences can always be increased by at least one. But although TV and Diagonal differ in this respect, there is a related feature which they share: whether or not there is a definite number of messages that can be transmitted in each depends not upon features of the code – the mathematical representations in TV or the grid and rules for Diagonal – but upon features of that which is coded, the TV picture on the screen and the language whose texts are coded.

Right at the start, then, we must note a clear disparity between codes and human languages, for every theorist of language maintains that it is a universal feature of human languages that there is no finite bound on the number of grammatical sentences that can be formed in a language. Moreover, this feature is standardly ascribed to a language not on the basis of the number of things that can be said in a language, the semantic content of its grammatical sentences, but on the basis of the structure of the syntactic rules of human languages.

Concerning the second noted feature of TV, absence of syntax, there is also in Diagonal no distinction between a well-formed message and an ill-formed one that can be made exclusively in terms of the code. In order to discern and describe such a distinction, reference must be made to the syntactic structure of some particular language whose sentences are coded. Any distinction between grammatical and ungrammatical strings that is applied to the coded text is there by proxy only, by extrapolation from the clean text. But the rules for encoding specify no particular language; just as any mathematical representation in TV may code an instant of some well-formed picture, any concatenation of pairs of letters of the alphabet in Diagonal may code a clean text, or part of one, in some language – including languages that are perhaps not known to us. To say that Diagonal has no syntax is not to deny either that a code has rules that are to be followed in encoding and decoding or that the encoder could make a mistake in applying the rules, for example, by substituting for two letters in the same row the two letters next to each on the left instead of those to the right. Such a mistake could be detected, however, only by a decoder who knows either what the clean text is or what the language of the clean text is. It could not be discerned from the code text alone nor from the code text plus the rules for encoding/decoding. These rules do not function in the same way as the syntax of a natural language. The syntax of a language exhibits a pattern of regular relations with the semantic content of its sentences: regular alterations of syntax result in regular alterations of meaning. So, the change in word order from 'The game is in the box' to 'The box is in the game' is an instance of a general syntactic-semantic correlation; the meanings of such sentence pairs differ in a regular way independently of the particular content of the sentences. But of course there is no regular correlation between the rules of Diagonal and the meanings of clean texts coded in Diagonal (which, *ex hypothesi*, can be in any language using the Roman alphabet). The rules of Diagonal are not rules over semantically or syntactically significant linguistic units; that is why one does not select letters of the alphabet as primitives for doing descriptive syntax or semantics of natural languages. Having said this, however, it should be acknowledged that there is a sense in which the rules for Diagonal could be said to be syntactic. This is a purely formal sense of 'syntax': they are syntactic in the sense that they specify transformations of concatenations of strings that can be described over and performed on shapes (of letters) in a purely mechanical way, at least in principle. But if we were to say that Diagonal has a 'syntax' in this sense, then its semantics would consist in the relevant interpretations of strings of shapes as strings of letters of the alphabet. However, these strings of letters would be, by themselves, without further semantic import, for they cannot be matched with words of a language unless the decoder knows which is the relevant language, so that the strings can be re-segmented into orthographic tokens of its words. Just as TV is insensitive to "real" pictures – arrays that we find pictorial – so is Diagonal insensitive to real words of a language and, in effect, makes no reference to them.[3] The rules of Diagonal refer only to strings of letters.

The third feature of TV noted was that the units of the code and the units of the picture must each be identifiable independently of one another by the encoder and the decoder; the units of the code cannot be consulted in order to determine what the units to be coded are and vice versa. The two sets of units stand to each other in one-to-one correlation; encoding and decoding are matching operations aimed at constructing a biunique correlation. Analogously, for Diagonal to be usable for encoding and decoding texts, the encoder must be able to identify the clean text, including its relevant units – letters and ordered pairs of letters – without consulting the code; and the decoder must be able to identify the code text, including its relevant units, without consulting either the particular clean text or the language of the clean text. I do not mean that each must know that the relevant units are letters and ordered pairs of letters without knowing Diagonal, but only that those units must be discernible by each independently of any biunique correlation set up by Diagonal for any operation of encoding and decoding to take place.

If our comparison of human languages with these simple examples of codes has until now seemed straightforward enough, complications loom with this third feature. To simplify matters, one obvious and unimportant disanalogy between human languages and our sample codes can be dispensed with. Both TV and Diagonal establish biunique correlations, correlations that are one-to-one. In this, I have followed Cherry's characterization of codes. Usually, however, a weaker condition is placed on codes. Abstract coding theorists, for example, take as their basic definition of a code one that imposes the more general feature of unique decipherability, treating biunique codes as a special kind. Certainly this is the course to take in assessing the characterization of languages as codes, since whatever it is that languages are supposed to code might, it seems, be capable of being encoded in different ways by the same language, while a code whose texts were not uniquely decipherable would seem no code at all. For such a "code" would be such that the coded text together with the code rules are insufficient to define a unique message. The results of "decoding" a message in such a "code" would vary independently of any features of the "code". In what respect would it be a code, then, rather than some other sort of phenomenon? Of course, if one supposes that everything in the universe is a "message" in some code or other, meaning by this merely that we can conceptualize it or learn something from it, then the code metaphor for languages becomes vacuous.

There are two additional features that any code that could be usable to encode and decode messages would seem obviously to require. First, the relevant correlation of units should remain unchanged from the time of encoding to the time of decoding; that is, the code must be stable across the relevant times. But also, both the units of what is to be encoded and the units of the code must be uniformly identifiable by encoders and decoders; if

I want to transmit a message to you in coded form with the result that you are able to decode the message in a successful communication, then you and I had better be in agreement about what the units of the code are as well as the units of what is coded.

Before continuing this explication and assessment of the code metaphor, let us pause and take stock of the features mentioned. Note that these are not offered as necessary and sufficient conditions for anything to be a code, nor as criteria; they are instead obvious features that codes share and so central to something's being a code that to say that human languages are codes must be to invoke some or all of them. On the other hand, if none of these features is invoked by the metaphor, then we would be advised to abandon the metaphor altogether. Here, then, is our inventory of characteristics. A code that is used to encode and decode messages is such that:

(1) it is uniquely decipherable;
(2) whether or not there is a definite number of messages that can be transmitted in it depends upon features of what is encoded rather than upon features of the code;
(3) it has no syntax independently of what it is used to encode;
(4) the units of what is to be encoded can be identified (that is, discerned) without consulting their code-correlates or the code in general;
(5) the units of the code can be identified (that is, discerned) without consulting their code-correlates;
(6) the relevant correlation of units remains unchanged from the time of encoding to the time of decoding;
(7) the units of what is to be encoded and the units of the code must be uniformly identifiable by encoders and decoders.

The reason for pursuing this metaphor in detail is that the respects in which human languages fail to resemble codes are very much respects by means of which human language confers on our species its cognitive distinctiveness. But this story cannot be told without first looking, briefly, at the number and kinds of blows that efforts to find code-correlata for various units of discourse have received in the not too distant past. These objections, however, have often been diffuse, displaying a frustrating

generality and leaving the reader to suspect that a mere preference for some other explanatory framework has predisposed the
critic. This history comes into sharper focus now, against the
background of the central characteristics of codes; for these criticisms can each now be understood as denying that human languages exhibit one or more of the features of codes listed above.
Most importantly, however, the transparency of the above code
examples will permit us to argue that the central problem with
any code theory of language is not that such theories cannot
perspicuously represent syntactic, semantic or pragmatic relations;
for they can. When that is all they aim to do, as it sometimes
certainly is, one should perhaps not call them "theories of language" but, apart from this, there is no problem. What will
emerge from our considerations as the central problem with all
code theories of language, even the most recent, is that they cannot satisfactorily account for language acquisition.

9   Referential Semantics: Breaking the Code?

Both Locke's (1706) doctrine that words "in their primary or
immediate signification, stand for nothing, but the Ideas, in the
mind of him that uses them," and Mill's (1872) view that words
are primarily names of things rather than ideas were efforts to
find some class of things to serve as code-correlata for words of
a language. In this century, both views were attacked as inadequate theories of linguistic meaning, Locke's in particular on the
ground that there is too much variety among the things that
different speakers of a language consider to be the conscious idea
for which any word stands for these to be considered to be the
meanings of words, if we grant that the word 'idea' itself has
some clearly identifiable referent.[4] Cast in terms of the code
metaphor, this problem with Locke's suggestion is that the units
he selects as code-correlata, ideas, do not exhibit feature (7) above,
they are not uniformly identifiable by encoders and decoders.[5]

Much of the subsequent history of semantics can be seen
as consisting of efforts to propose some satisfactory alternative
to private, language-independent, psychological ideas as the

code-correlata for linguistic units. Thoughts, meanings, facts, states of affairs, propositions, situations, and possible worlds are some of the things that have been proposed as non-psychological, publicly identifiable items with the requisite uniformity throughout a population. Ryle (1971, p. 352ff.) gave the following criticism of Mill's thesis: if words are names of things then a sentence is a list of names; but a sentence can be true or false while a list cannot. Hence, a sentence is not a list of names and words are not names of things.

Ryle's criticism, too, can be made more precise in terms of the features of codes outlined above, specifically, feature (3): a coded message has no syntax independently of its clean text. Any syntax that the coded message can be said to have, it has only parasitically upon the syntax of the message it encodes. Only sentences that have the syntax of an assertion can be true or false; nor is there any predication without syntax. However, the things named by a list do not generally have any syntax to contribute to the list, and so not the syntax of an assertion. Since there is no truth without assertion and no assertion without syntax, and since sentences can be true (or false), sentences cannot be lists of names.

The naive coding theories of Locke and Mill took different types of things to be the fundamental non-linguistic units with which linguistic units are correlated, mental ideas and extra-mental things. Subsequent theorists vacillated between these two extremes and sometimes proposed a type of correlatum that was not clearly of either sort, such as sense-data. The early conceptions of philosophical and logical analysis proposed by Russell and Moore incorporated more sophisticated coding theories of human language. But the picture becomes increasingly complicated here by the, often explicit, aim of Russell and others to describe human language as it ought to be, in accordance with their conception of the constraints on what humans could know, rather than as it is and subject to all the cognitive fallibility to which humans are heir. So, in the works of Russell, Carnap and others, the general theory of human language merges with proposals for the ideal language of science – the language that would express with perfect clarity what humans really know, and no more than that. This would be a language purged of all spurious conceptions,

conceptions that did not logically deconstruct into units that were simply correlated with the irreducibly known. Russell's conception of languages as codes is clearest when he characterizes his referential semantics for an ideal language in his lectures on logical atomism and philosophical analysis:

> All analysis is only possible in regard to what is complex, and it always depends, in the last analysis, upon direct acquaintance with the objects which are the meanings of certain simple symbols. . . . In a logically perfect language the words in a proposition would correspond one by one with the components of the corresponding fact, with the exception of such words as 'or', 'not', 'if', 'then', which have a different function. In a logically perfect language, there will be one word and no more for every simple object, and everything that is not simple will be expressed by a combination of words, a combination derived, of course, from the words for each simple component. A language of that sort will be completely analytic, and will show at a glance the logical structure of the facts asserted or denied.   (Russell, 1956, pp. 194, 197–8)

The language that Russell envisages is not only a uniquely decipherable code, it is apparently also a biunique code, and one whose syntax will be derived from what it codes, the "logical structure of facts". Russell realized that syntactic structures can themselves be, in some sense, informative and that an adequate account of language must account for those information-bearing structures. The "true" structures, then, are the ones to be discovered by a perfected science and reflected in a logically perfect language through its sentential structures, which will be isomorphic with those discovered structures in the world.

The "picture theory of language" of Wittgenstein's *Tractatus* (1922) has been read along similar lines, certainly by Russell who credited Wittgenstein (who repudiated the credit) with ideas contained in Russell's "Lectures on Logical Atomism".[6] But there is another construal of Wittgenstein's reflections on language and referential semantics in the *Tractatus*, a construal that places his later *Philosophical Investigations* (1953) in a coherent relation to the earlier work. On this construal, the Wittgenstein of the *Tractatus* saw something puzzling in the conception of a language, even a logically perfect language, as a code. What he saw was that if a human language is a code then we can never, in a sense, decipher it; we can never write the clean text. If a language is a code, then there must be code units, simple signs or names that code-correlate with simple objects. If an elementary proposition/sentence is a code text for (a picture of) a state of affairs that engages only simple objects, then, once we have analysed a situation and arrived at an elementary proposition that codes or pictures it, we cannot then decode *that* proposition in language. Ultimately, any candidate for a clean text must be non-linguistic, something that might, perhaps, be grasped and coded but that cannot be spoken. Furthermore, we cannot write down the coding rules because, since we cannot write down the objects themselves with which the simple names correlate, we cannot write down the correlation that the purported code sets up. Any code conception of a language, such as a referential semantics presents, entails that there are simple units of the language that are simply correlated with the items for which they are the code names; so any code conception of a language entails a version of atomism, at least one of linguistic atomism. If the language is supposed also to reflect the human epistemic condition relative to the world along the lines that Russell envisaged for an idealized language of science, then it would seem that humans could never fully understand that epistemic condition since they could never articulate crucial parts of the code.

On this interpretation, then, a principal thesis of the *Tractatus* is the hypothetical one: If human languages, even a logically perfect one that might be spoken by scientists privy to a perfected empirical science, are codes, then we can never decipher their coded messages. And this would mean that we could never fully conceptualize the relationship established or exemplified by a language. But if having an adequate philosophical understanding of human knowledge, human language, and the world requires arriving at the correct, ultimate, and unique description of these things and their relations to one another, which is what it did mean to Russell, Carnap and others, then such understanding is not attainable.

If the *Investigations* can be said to have an overriding, albeit underlying, thesis, it is that, contrary to the above conclusion, an understanding of human knowledge, language, and the world is attainable. The *Investigations* seeks to reveal the errors in the grounds on which this seemed unattainable. And one major source of these errors is the conception of human natural languages that was assumed. On the account here suggested, then, the *Investigations* is not in conflict with the conditional thesis of the *Tractatus*. Rather, it argues for the falsehood of the antecedent of that conditional. The critique of referential semantics that runs throughout the *Investigations* constitutes an implicit argument that human languages are not codes. Wittgenstein very likely despaired of the possibility of articulating explicitly either the argument from referential semantics to the opacity, to us, of our own epistemic condition, or the subsequent argument in the *Investigations* that a referential semantics cannot provide a naturalistic account of human languages. Perhaps those who have developed so extensively the code metaphor for languages have placed us in a better situation.

9.1   The Language Acquisition Problem

The reflections that culminated in the *Investigations* follow quite naturally from the Tractarian argument as construed above. If we who are mature users of a language can do nothing that would count as deciphering the elementary "coded messages" of a natural language, whatever they are supposed to be, if we cannot conceptualize the "clean text" except as it is coded, then how can a prelinguistic child be supposed to be able to do just that, to conceptualize an uncoded clean text? The things that are presumed to code-correlate with the simplest code names of a language, if a language is a code, would need to be identified by the child, and uniformly by other pre-linguistic children and the whole language community, independently of the code, and stably over time and among individual "encoders" and "decoders", in accordance with features (4), (6), and (7) of codes. Of course, there aren't really any proper "decoders" of the simplest code names even in the mature population of language users according to the hypothetical argument above, so if, *per impossibile*, the pre-linguistic child were identifying items independently of the language for the simplest code names to name and in learning the language as a code, *we* could never ascertain this. But this last point is not clearly to be found in the *Investigations*.

The argument of the *Investigations* that human languages are not codes has this structure. If human languages are codes, then to learn one requires identifying its basic code-correlata independently of the language – that is, without consulting the purported code – and with the requisite stability over time and uniformity among speakers. And if human languages are codes, then their basic code-correlata are either extra-mental things such as physical objects and properties, or mental things like sense-data, thoughts, pains, and intentions. But there is no conceivable way for the pre-linguistic child to identify any items that are plausible code-correlata of either sort both independently of the language and with the requisite stability over time and uniformity among speakers. In our terms, features (4), (6), and (7) cannot be instantiated by what the child does. So, if human languages are codes, a child cannot learn one. But children do learn (acquire, achieve, . . .) languages. Hence, they are not codes.

There are two parts to the argument, one for the possibility that the basic code-correlata are extra-mental things and one for the possibility that the basic code-correlata are mental things. First, if the basic code-correlata are extra-mental things, natural candidates are things that correlate with some subclass of common nouns. Virtually all theories of referential semantics in the history supposed this. And ostension was the only candidate in that history for a procedure whereby a specific referent was presumed to be selected. Wittgenstein's discussions of ostensive definition aim to show that ostension alone can never identify a basic code-correlatum that will have the requisite stability and uniformity for it to serve as the uniquely deciphering correlate of any expression in the language. The classic passages of the critique begin with *PI* 26, "One thinks that learning language consists in giving names to objects" (Wittgenstein, 1953, p. 12), and the general trouble with that view of initial language acquisition is described as the fact that "an ostensive definition can be variously interpreted in *every* case" (ibid., 28, p. 14), unless, of course, it is accompanied by a verbal characterization of the object in terms of some classifier such as "This color is called 'blue'", "This number is called 'two' ". But, then, one must already know the meaning of these classifiers to understand the new word being defined ostensively, so these cases cannot serve to explain language acquisition (ibid., 29, p. 14). Ostension alone cannot serve to establish the alleged correlation because there are no primitive (semantic) objects with the requisite features to stand as code correlates that are identifiable without consulting the language. Hence a language cannot be learned as a code for basic units that are extra-mental things.

The arguments implicit in the *Investigations* for the conclusion that a human language cannot be learned as a code whose basic code correlates are mental things likewise argue that there are no mental phenomena that can be identified independently of consulting the language that have the relevant stability and uniformity necessary for them to serve as such basic units. "When one says 'He gave a name to his sensation' one forgets that a great deal of stage-setting in the language is presupposed if the mere act of naming is to make sense. And when we speak of someone's having given a name to pain, what is presupposed is the existence of the grammar of the word 'pain'; it shews the post where the new word is stationed" (ibid., 257, p. 92). The much-attended Private Language Argument is an appealing *Gedanken*-experiment employed to the same end, to wit, to support the conclusion that nothing can be introspectively identified independently of the language that has the requisite stability and uniformities to enable it to serve as a basic code corelatum in the learning of a language. Since this is a negative existential conclusion that cannot be definitely established by an inspection of instances alone, Wittgenstein supplements his case-by-case inventory of possible candidates among mental things (thoughts, intentions, sense-data, . . .) with such an experiment.

Since the time of Wittgenstein's running of these arguments against a coding conception of human languages, a multitude of empirical research and experimental data has led researchers in the psychology of linguistic reference to similar conclusions. But the empirical task and the interpretations of its results have not been free from debate.

10 The New Code Theory

The principal targets of Wittgenstein's critique were Associationist theories of language that have always dominated the Empiricist tradition. The most recent code theory of human language is the one with which this chapter began, the Nativist account. On this account, a human language codes another language that is internal to the organism; learning a language is learning which predicates of the internal language are to be coded by which predicates of the human language (Fodor, 1975). Here is the argument offered in support of this view. When a child learns a first human language, what it learns is to pair the predicates of that language with something like a coextensive concept, via a truth rule perhaps; for example, the predicate 'ball' and its concept, F, via the rule:

$\langle y$ is a ball$\rangle$ is true if and only if x is F.

But, the argument continues, no one can give an explanation of how a child could acquire, by learning, both the units paired and the correct correlation. An explanation is possible only if we assume that the child already has the concept F, waiting inside as it were, ready to be so paired (Fodor, 1975).

It may be unfair to allude to this argument without reviewing the climate in linguistic theory at the time that it was devised. At that time it was widely accepted among theorists both that knowing a language consists in knowing rules for pairing syntactic structures with semantic structures and that these rules provide semantic representations of the predicates that occur in sentences of a language, representations that were understood as very much like necessary and sufficient conditions for the application of those predicates (Chomsky, 1965; Katz and Fodor, 1964). Chomsky's thesis that humans have innate knowledge of the universal grammar of human languages had also been advanced on the grounds that a competent speaker of a language displays a knowledge of syntax that could not have been learned (Chomsky, 1965). Additionally, the efforts of Davidson to account for meaning in natural languages by applying Tarski's "semantic conception of truth", originally formulated for formal languages, to human languages appeared to be meeting widespread acceptance (Davidson, 1967; Tarski, 1944). In such a theoretical climate, perhaps it was inevitable that the thesis should have been advanced that the semantics of human languages too are innate, with the semantics described as consisting of "T-sentences" for the language in question. Nevertheless, it is important to assess this theory not only because of its obvious appeal to those who seek a computational theory of human mentality but especially because it is a theory that does not permit an answer to the questions that this study raises. For it is a theory that precludes those questions.

The main problem with the new code theory – both pointed out in critique (Harnad, 1987a) and boasted of in praise (Fodor, 1987) – is that it is intrinsically incapable of verification, confirmation, falsification, or disconfirmation. But it is revealing, nevertheless, to assess it also in terms of the features of codes developed in this chapter and the classic criticisms of conceiving of languages as codes. The new coding theory is not open to Wittgenstein's criticism that one must consult the code (the human language to be learned) in order to determine what the units are of the internal language that is to be coded by it. For, on this version, the organism is innately structured so as to be able, prior to learning the human language, to distinguish among and to use in thought the units of the innate language of thought that are subsequently encoded by the learned language. The Wittgensteinian argument against the view that human languages code mental things understandably presumed that any such mental things would be phenomena, things of which one is aware. But the language of thought hypothesis does not propose that the alleged mental items that a learned language codes are phenomena of which we are (prelinguistically, at any rate) conscious.

The new coding theory *is* open to the objection, however, that one would have to consult the "clean text", that is, the language of thought that the human language is supposed to encode, in order to discern the units of the code itself; to discern, that is, the units of the external language to be learned. This is no mere technical objection based on one, admittedly simple, notion of what a code is. Rather, what underlies the objection is the fact that, when we learn a word, 'ball' for example, we normally acquire not only the concept of a ball but we (begin to) acquire the concept of the word 'ball' as well; indeed, for every concept correlated with a word of a human language, there is also the concept of that word. So, the general argument above given to support this coding view would have to apply also to every word of every human language that can be learned. That is, for each word of a language that humans acquire a concept of, we must suppose that the human learns to pair the concept of the word with a coextensive concept, via a truth-rule perhaps; for example, the predicate 'the word "ball"' and its concept G via the rule:

$\langle y$ is the word 'ball'$\rangle$ is true if and only if x is G.

By parity of argument, we would have to conclude that the child has an innate knowledge of a coextensive concept for every word of every human language; which is to say, an innate knowledge of the units of the external code that it learns. On this argument, it seems that the child does not even learn the learned language, the alleged code. Since children do obviously acquire their first human language – no one is arguing that English, or Hebrew, or . . . , is innate – the argument must be faulty.

Nor will it do to counter this objection by claiming either that speakers of a language need have no (metalinguistic) concepts for the words of a language in order to have concepts for what the words mean or refer to, or that a language learner can do without specific concepts for each word in favor of a small number of concepts for, say, the phonemes of the language together with one concept of a word. For, to the first counter, while there is no logical necessity to have, for example, the concept of the word 'ball' in order to have the concept of a ball, nevertheless, to use the English word 'ball' correctly it is necessary to be able to distinguish that word from others, to reidentify successive occurrences of that word and, in general, to behave with respect to *that word* in ways that are associated with having attained the relevant concept of that word. And, to the second counter, it need only be pointed out that phoneme identification is made by speakers of a language quite standardly on the basis of such higher-order discriminations as which word the putative phoneme is a constituent of and what the word means, as revealed by its syntactic, semantic, and pragmatic contexts of occurrence. One cannot identify the phonemes of a language (as phonemes of that language) without knowing words of the language. In fact, it is in part a computer's inability to achieve these competencies, banal for humans, that accounts for its low general verbal aptitude.

11   Mature Competency and Language Learning

It is important to note that none of the above argues that we who are mature speakers of a language cannot select some extra-linguistic items, items that we consider to be part of the physical world, for example, and map them onto simple or complex expressions of our language. Indeed we do this all the time whenever we name or describe extra-linguistic physical things. It is my cat that I named "Isis". So, from within a language it is not only quite possible to treat a language as a code but for some purposes it may be most efficient to think of languages as codes, for example, for purposes of computer modelling of what a mature speaker does, a speaker with a large store of world-knowledge of a propositional sort who is positioned within a language.[7] But it does not follow that those computational processes perspicuously represent or reveal the processes involved in initial language acquisition. We must distinguish, then, models of mature speech from models of language acquisition.

I have argued in this chapter that human languages are not codes; in particular, that human languages could not be learned as codes on or for something else. But just now I have acknowledged that mature discourse might be perspicuously represented as a code. This seems puzzling. How can a process that is not fundamentally a coding process, that is, language learning, result in a product that can be construed as a code? The new coding theory of human language presents a challenge, for the argument advanced for it is that its account of what the language learner learns and its account of how this learning takes place are the only accounts available. I propose to turn now to this puzzle and to take up that challenge.

It is standard today to suppose, with Fodor, that a theory of language acquisition must follow upon a theory of mature linguistic competence that is arrived at independently of developmental considerations and that specifies in detail what it is that is acquired. An alternative approach suggested by Vygotsky, among others, has been widely ignored: "The result of development will be neither a purely psychological structure such as descriptive psychology considers the result to be, nor a simple sum of elementary processes such as associationistic psychology saw it, but a qualitatively new form that appears in the process of development" (Vygotsky, 1978, p. 65).

Notes

1 Macnamara (1986), however, explicitly rejects the claim, which he attributes to Chomsky, that pre-linguistic children have beliefs.
2 See, e.g., Shannon and Weaver, 1964; for caveats on analogous extrapolations, see Berlinski, 1976.
3 Compare Pylyshyn (1984, p. 65): "It is a general property of events and physical objects that if they are instances (token occurrences) of a *code* that designates something extrinsic to the physical system (that is, which is given a semantic interpretation), then, even though physical laws govern the properties of the *instances* (for example, their shape and succession if they are generated mechanically), the relationship among the events *as* codes must be stated in the form of rules that depend on what they are codes *for*. Anticipating an example used in chapter 7, I point out that patterns of Morse code follow rules of spelling because they are codes for letters. To express this, however, we must refer to what the codes represent: letters."
4 Hacking (1975) has argued persuasively that Locke could have had no conception of and hence no theory of linguistic meaning. This question, however, is largely irrelevant to the issue of this section, which is concerned rather with Locke's account of human language as a code on non-linguistic mental phenomena quite independently of whether Locke had a theory of meaning.
5 Alston (1964) argues, in effect, that because 'idea' is hopelessly vague, Locke's proposal is untestable, but that if we substitute 'images' for 'ideas' then empirical evidence shows the proposal to be false. Brown (1958) surveys empirical evidence supporting this conclusion about images.

6   Russell acknowledged in his preface to the published lectures that Wittgenstein had pointed out to him that his account, generating propositions from knowledge by acquaintance with the objects that are the components of simple facts, failed to sustain an account of false propositions – there being no false facts, hence none that could generate false propositions.

7   We may profit from treating language as a code in accounts also of cognitive therapy and psychoanalysis, as Edward Casey has suggested to me; although I am inclined towards a slightly different explanation of these activities, one whose basic relation is analogy rather than equivalence.

3 Language Entry

The speech skills have a tremendous potential for assisting the formation of non-linguistic categories. The total list of such categories that a child must learn is a cognitive inventory of his culture. Speech, therefore, is the principal instrument of cognitive socialization.

Roger Brown, Words and Things

12 Linguistic Constructionalism

The following supposition seems warranted: There is no correlation of the semantic elements of a language with items in the world that are uniformly identifiable by random members of a language community independently of and prior to the acquisition of that language. Vast amounts of empirical evidence and philosophical analysis lead us to make this supposition. If this is the case, then no referential semantics can explain language acquisition even though different versions of referential semantics may provide models of large parts of the mature speaker's linguistic ability and behavior. That is, if this supposition is correct, then language acquisition is not fundamentally a matter of breaking a code, of successfully achieving by means of a matching operation a unique correlation of semantic units of a language with independently identified elements of the world or of the mind, or vice versa. While some such correlation may be part of the product of language acquisition, thinking of language learning as code-breaking does not provide a sufficiently perspicuous characterization of the product to serve as the model for a theory of language learning. This suggestion is at first puzzling. How can a result that is capable of being modelled by correlational structures be the product of a process that is not basically correlational? The answer that will be proposed here is that the resulting correlations are between items each of which is partly constructed by the process itself of learning a language.

If this supposition is correct, then the process of language acquisition is also entirely different from what has been proposed overwhelmingly to date in many variations, no one of which has been able to represent that process satisfactorily. A different model of what occurs in language learning is required. I propose shortly to describe a plausible alternative structure. This structure is suggested by, indeed virtually falls out of, recent research in developmental psycholinguistics. Before describing this alternative structure, however, it is useful to consider by way of a deeper diagnosis than the foregoing discussion of coding conceptions provides why current conceptions of human language fail to accommodate, or even to address, the desiderata for a theory of human language described in chapter 1.

13   The Fallacy of Linguistic Supervenience

There is a research program widely underway that I shall call the Linguistic Supervenience Program. A property of a product is said to supervene upon a process if and only if the process causally, logically, or computationally necessitates that the product have that property. So, for example, heat might be thought to supervene upon a certain process involving the motion of molecules; fatigue, upon certain metabolic processes. In the propositional calculus, validity of an inference is a property that supervenes upon certain logical operations (that is, upon the application or applicability of those operations).

In this characterization, a non-standard use of 'supervenience' is adopted. The concept was originally used informally to explain relations between ethical and aesthetic properties, such as *good* and *beautiful*, and the physically describable properties of things said to be good or beautiful (Hare, 1952; Sibley, 1959); the former were said to "supervene" on the latter. Since that time, formally different concepts of supervenience have been considered, often in discussions of relations between "the physical" and "the mental" (Kim, 1978; 1984; and Horgan, 1987). Most recently, the concept has been invoked in the course of discussing questions about the "individualism" of "mental content" (Burge, 1986; and Davies, 1991).[1]

There are several reasons for departing from the conventions used in these contexts in the present case. First, it would be question-begging to adopt the distinction between physical properties and mental properties implicit in these inquiries; it would be to presume that an ontological taxonomy I am at pains to avoid is clear. But also, characterizing the relation of supervenience as between "processes internal to the individual" and "products of those processes", rather than as one between two kinds of properties, permits the inclusion of both physicalistic and mentalistic accounts as instances of the alleged fallacy. Finally, the current concern of this essay, as will be seen shortly, is the relation between developmental processes of language acquisition and linguistic competence – a product of those processes – rather than one between two kinds of properties.

As I conceive it, the task of the Linguistic Supervenience Program is to describe those causal, logical, or computational structures internal to the individual which account for, by necessitating, mature language competence. Thus, verbal fluency is supposed by this program to supervene upon processes that are *internal to the individual*; a tiny amount of exposure to language-using others in very early childhood is supposed necessary merely to trigger into action the relevant internal structures and processes upon which mature fluency is thought to supervene. I think that one major reason why current theories of human language do not meet the desiderata for a theory of human language described in chapter 1 is that they accept a false assumption that is entrenched in this program. This is the assumption that the features of a model of mature discourse supervene upon causal, logical or computational processes within the individual language learner.[2] For example, Richard Montague's denotational semantics models mature discourse by "assigning extra-linguistic entities to all expressions involved in the generation of sentences . . . in such a way that (a) the assignment to a compound will be a function of the entities assigned to its components and (b) the truth value of a sentence can be determined from the entity assigned to it" (Montague, 1974). It would be an instance of the fallacy of linguistic supervenience to suppose that a realistic account of language learning will show how these features of the model are causal, logical, or computational products of what goes on within the individual during the process of language learning.

That a property of normal discourse may not supervene on processes internal to the language learner is neither puzzling nor mysterious. Even in the case of purely physical processes, properties of a product are expected to be fully explained by a description of its generative process only to the extent that the process can reasonably be treated as taking place within a closed system. Experimental physics can construct virtual closed systems within which products and their processes can be scrupulously monitored in isolation from unknown variables that might intervene between process and product. However, this experimental cleanliness is nowhere else to be observed, not even in equally fastidious non-human sciences. In geology and astrophysics, for example, there is always the possibility of hidden and unknown variables influencing a product, even in a regular way, and resulting in the product's having a property that is not accounted for by the process that brought about the product. We allow that a product may have qualities that do not supervene upon the physical causal history of the product. Neither is this allowance mysterious nor metaphysically suspect. In fact, it is our typical cognitive relation to events in our environment. It is typical also of our understanding of behavioral products and their underlying generative histories. Here too, a good description of the product may refer to qualities it has which do not supervene upon the causal processes that underly it. The result may have qualities that the "cause" neither has nor gives to it; it may have these as a result of its relations to things outside of the individual agent who nevertheless brought it about.

Although it is far less complicated than linguistic behavior, the example of drivers acting in accordance with motor vehicle laws sustains the appropriate analogy. Their behavior is, by and large, lawful, although in fact many drivers do not know the laws to which their behavior conforms. Those who don't have propositional knowledge of these laws may tend to violate them more often than those who do, but then again they may not. They may realize that they risk personal harm and the frustration of their own goals in violating the motor vehicle laws independently of whether they conceptualize those laws. For they may be aware only of regularities in the behavior of other drivers, much as one is aware of the behavior of other pedestrians and avoids collision with them. That the laws have been articulated and are known by some probably helps to maintain the degree of regularity in driving behavior that there is, but drivers may conform to the laws in their driving behavior without knowing what they are or even that they exist. Isomorphisms may thus be sustained between the behaviors of drivers and the external conditions of driving that are encompassed by the laws without supposing individual knowledge of the laws to account for the observed regularities. If there were no such laws, or if no one knew them, then maybe the situation would be different. But an individual's driving behavior (the product) may be in accordance with the law (correct description of the product) even though this feature of the behavior does not supervene upon the causal history of the individual's behavior or upon any processes internal to the individual. That the behavior is in accord with the laws is a relational feature of the resultant behavior with the motor vehicle law, with other drivers, with the behavior and knowledge of other drivers, and so forth.

The moral is that we should not suppose that an accurate description of a product refers only to properties that are explicable in terms of what we understand to be the causal history of that product. Such supervenience of products upon processes assumes ideal conditions of inquiry and a closed system under perfect observation by a disinterested non-participant in the system.[3] These are conditions that our human cognitive limitations of finitude and perspective contravene in all but the most restricted domains of inquiry. Physics presents a model of such inquiry to us, but it is a model that we have constructed and it cannot alter our cognitive limitations, although it may confuse us about the aims of our inquiries. Thus we may have excellent descriptions and models of mature discourse that refer to properties that do not supervene upon processes wholly internal to the language learner. The code-like correlation between words and extra-linguistic things that mature discourse exhibits is, I propose, such a property. Humans are in a particularly disadvantageous position with respect to appreciating the fallacy of supervenience when it occurs in theorizing about language because, for competent speakers, our language is often the form of our conceptualization. The result is that it is literally second nature for us to project our own linguistic competencies upon others, and upon our earlier selves (cf. Wittgenstein, 1953, 104, p. 46).

14   Semantic Theory and Language Learning

The focus nowadays in the theory of language has been semantic theory and a number of such theories, some competing, some complementary, have been offered. Another reason why current conceptions of human language fail to address the desiderata for a theory of language is that the fallacy of supervenience has proliferated with the help of a faulty conception of the relationship between semantic theory and language learning. That conception is that facts about language learning are largely irrelevant to semantic theory.

Historically, this belief resulted from a confluence of several different sources. One was the trend toward anti-psychologism in philosophy, the original home of semantic theory. By "anti-psychologism" here, I mean the belief that one finds in, for example, Frege and Russell, that psychological issues and claims are irrelevant to philosophy. It appealed especially to those who thought philosophy to be concerned only with *a priori* or conceptual truths.

Another source of the doctrine divorcing language learning from semantic theory was the rich development of concepts of formal languages in the philosophy of mathematics and in philosophy of science during the first half of this century, and the basic role of set theory in this development. Formal languages were conceived as set-theoretic structures whose properties were open to rigorous analysis. What will emerge in the second part of this chapter is that language acquisition proceeds in accordance with processes and operations that do not seem to be intrinsically set-theoretical.

Details of these origins need not concern us here. Instead, I shall review briefly one direction in which semantic theory has developed, in linguistics and in philosophy, to exclude data about language acquisition.

We can accept the characterization of semantics given by Barwise and Perry (1983, p. 27): "Semantics is the study of linguistic meaning, of the relationships that hold between expressions of language and things in the world." Current approaches to semantic theory aim to conduct this study in precise ways by making use of various structures provided by mathematics and logic. In particular, model-theoretic semantics uses the formal apparatus of model theory, that part of logic concerned with the relation between the expressions of mathematical discourse and the mathematical structures they describe. Montague grammar is one such construction designed to apply to (a part of) natural languages. Barwise and Perry offer a different model-theoretic semantics for natural languages designed to be more naturalistic, or ecological as they say, than Montague's formal semantics. In addition to such purely formal semantics, there have been several attempts to construct accounts of natural language semantics that I shall call "quasi-formal". Whereas a formal semantics has a precise formal structure that is made explicit by giving a list of primitive terms or concepts that will be taken as undefined, an explicit characterization of basic structures, and an explicit articulation of the operations that may be applied to those terms and structures in order to generate other terms and structures, a quasi-formal semantics is designed to describe a process or structure as effectively computable (this feature it shares with formal semantics) but it does this only implicitly rather than explicitly. Usually, a quasi-formal semantics takes the apparatus of some formal theory and tries to show how that apparatus can be applied to some real-world phenomenon to account for certain problematic or poorly understood features of that phenomenon. So, I count Dretske's (1981) brilliant application of the concepts of Information Theory to problems about perception, knowledge, and belief as a quasi-formal semantics, as well as Johnson-Laird's (1983) use of Montague semantics in his account of cognitive processes and Fodor's (1975) appeals to the structures in Davidson's truth-based semantics to explain linguistic competence. Sometimes, as in the case of Dretske's theory, a quasi-formal semantics is an attempt to work out a new application of a prior application of a formal theory, an extension of the old application with the focus on showing how the former application fits the new domain and solves (or represents more perspicuously) problems within the new domain of application. Sometimes, it is an attempt to show how a phenomenon, construed by some application of the parent formalism, presents a problem to our understanding which requires some solution, as is the case in Fodor's characterization of linguistic competence as knowledge of a truth definition for the language of competence.

Although semantics thus construed is only a part of the theory of human language, it is a crucial part and one where the desiderata of a theory of language might be expected to be met to some degree. At least, a semantic theory should cohere with a general account of language that satisfies those desiderata; but it is to be hoped that a semantic theory will do more, that it will shed some good light on the aspects of human language that those desiderata capture. Alas, however, current offerings of semantic theories fall far short of these hopes; indeed, many of them seem to construe human language in a way that is altogether incompatible with the satisfaction of those desiderata. I think that the recent history of semantics reveals why there is such a large gap between those desiderata and current semantic theories and goes some way, as well, towards explaining the attraction that the fallacy of linguistic supervenience has in semantic theorizing.

14.1   The Standard Paradigm

The classic paradigm for construing the relative locations of semantic theory and the theory of language learning is Chomsky's (1965) tripartite structure: a Competence Model represents the linguistic knowledge of the ideal speaker–hearer; a Performance Model represents the psychological processes actually employed in speaker–hearer verbal behavior; the Language Acquisition Device (LAD) is the mechanical structure, presumed innate, which subtends language learning. On this paradigm, a semantic theory is contained in the competence model. In principle, each of these levels was construed as equally constraining the other, but the assumption of the innateness of the LAD resulted in its being presumed to contribute one overriding constraint.

Within this classic model, it is assumed that the acquisition of a language is the result of a language-specific innate disposition, a device hard-wired into the organism at birth and requiring minimal physical maturation plus a tiny amount of experiential input to be "triggered". A result of this assumption is that the LAD was construed as exercising a considerable constraint upon both competence models and performance models, the constraint that there is a *uniquely correct* competence model and performance model. These would be the unique models that *correctly* characterize the product of the LAD when it is triggered by its appropriate stimuli and processed through the mechanisms whereby verbal performance issues. This is indeed a very large constraint.[4]

On the other hand, the assumption of the innateness of the LAD also led to the conclusion that its structure can be understood only *after* we have arrived at the unique competence model and, then, the correct performance model (constrained in all respects by the correct competence model but only in principle by the LAD). That is, the LAD will be exactly specified only by the competence model. Its specifications are those of whatever mechanism is required to subtend the unique structure that the competence model describes. The LAD is innate, but not capable of being understood by looking directly at neuronal activity. Hence, all we can know about it is what the competence model specifies that it equips the organism to learn.

On this paradigm, competence models were construed as, for all theoretical purposes, distinct from and uninformed by data about language learning (it's too quick a process, its input too impoverished), or even about verbal performance.[5] Although it encouraged rich, fruitful research into linguistic structures in search of the, presumed unique, correct theory of language, it placed substantive questions about whether and how cognitive development might be altered during the period of language acquisition, not merely far in the background, but *out of the picture*. Such concerns were dismissed as Piagetian, with the understanding that Piaget did not appreciate the new Rationalist discovery, being as syntactically naive as Skinner had been. The period of language "learning" had been argued to be very brief, full competence almost immediately following upon minimal physical maturation. On this paradigm, the only developmental data relevant to the theory of language would be data about the order of acquisition of certain linguistic competencies, semantic or syntactic, insofar as such data might shed light on the theory of universals of language. What the basic, innate linguistic structures are could not be found from developmental studies but only from the competence model of the mature speaker-hearer.

This notion of a competence model was, of course, tailor-made for the application of formal models of the sort developed in mathematics – in particular, set-theoretical models. When semantics was added to the basis of a transformational grammar, formerly conceived as purely syntactic, the form it took was very similar to that of the formal languages that had been designed early in this century by the positivists seeking to describe an ideal language of science. There were primitive terms that would correspond to the data of sense, and complex terms defined in terms of these primitives (see, for example, Katz and Fodor, 1964). The syntactic innateness hypothesis, as well as the later move to construe deep structure as logical form (Lycan, 1984; Macnamara, 1986), paralleled the efforts of the earlier logical constructionalists to describe formally specifiable rules for generating all desired propositions or expressions of the system (desired because scientific, or empirically meaningful, or . . .) from the primitive basis, the basic terms and structures (see, for example, Carnap, 1928; Goodman, 1951).

Within the Chomskian framework, then, the introduction of formal models of linguistic structures suited both the abstract character of the sought competence model and the assumption implicit in it that the knowledge represented by the competence model is innate. Innate knowledge of the semantic or syntactic structures of language would have to be transmitted organically, and so by means of structures.

Gradually, we have seen the application of formal models extended to other types of cognitive structures than linguistic ones, and the notion of semantics has broadened in psychology to include these non-linguistic structures (see, for example, Johnson-Laird, 1983). Of couse, efforts to develop formalisms in psychology had also been pursued quite independently of the Chomskian framework or its linguistic subject (see, for example, Miller, 1969), often in the course of pursuing for psychology the rigor found in physics. Nevertheless, the standard paradigm just described for construing the relation between semantic theory and language acquisition – reinforced perhaps by residual positivism (often expressed as rabid materialism) and encouraged by advances in machine and biological technologies as well as success in computer simulation of cognitive tasks – has, I think, led the way to theories of linguistic semantics that do not answer to any of the three desiderata for a theory of human language mentioned at the outset. That is, I think that one reason why current semantic theories do not shed any light on those issues is related to the dismissal of first-language learning as a mere developmental topic which is of no relevance to a theory of linguistic competence; and that a framework of formal semantics may have assisted in this oversight. To put the matter in yet a different way, I think that we have several elegant theories of (linguistic) semantic competence, formal as well as quasi-formal, which conflict with certain facts about language learning. If those facts were taken into account as data that a semantic theory should accommodate, then a theory that would go some way towards satisfying the desiderata mentioned might be possible.

Formal semantic theories have not aimed at representing realistically any facts about language acquisition, although some of the quasi-formal ones have. And all of them, formal and quasi-formal, ignore certain facts about language learning that emerge from developmental studies. Insofar as these semantic theories are understood as competence models that are related to models of language learning in accordance with the now classic paradigm of that relation, they conflict with those facts. Of course, insofar as they aim to be competence models alone, abstracted from any implicit or explicit claims about language learning, then they are not to be charged with this conflict, although one must then address questions about the basis for evaluating competing semantic theories of such an abstract sort.

15   Reconceptualizing Language Acquisition

I want now to describe certain specific and important facts about language learning that virtually all current semantic theories fail to represent. The particular mismatch between the structures that these theories present to us and these facts about language learning contributes in particular to their failure to meet the desideratum that a theory of human language should be anthropocentric in the sense explained in chapter 1, that is, that such a theory should sustain an account of the species-specific cognitive adaptive utility of human language. The facts about language learning that I shall describe are, briefly, these: that it takes much longer than assumed by the classic paradigm; and that it involves the acquisition of cognitive structures that are fundamentally unlike the structures that are evidenced in the behavior of non-human animals.

16   How Long Does It Take?

Developmental studies of language learning show that abilities to make numerous general semantic and syntactic distinctions – for example, to recognize ungrammatical sentences, ambiguous syntax, synonymous pairs of sentences; to comprehend riddles – emerge between the ages of five and twelve, with apparent peaks at ages six and eight; for riddles, between ten and twelve (see Tunmer and Grieve, 1984, for a summary of data). These studies are not individually conclusive; some incompetencies can, for example, be attributed to excessive demands upon limited memory. But together they make a strong case that full competence is both more gradual and takes much longer than the early nativist arguments claimed (suddenly, and between $2\frac{1}{2}$ and 5 years of age), and these studies show that there are sudden advances in these competencies at middle childhood. The most interesting studies about the character of early language are those of Jeremy Anglin and Frank Keil on the acquisition of general terms. It will be argued below that these studies reveal changes in what is clearly a cognitive competence that is interdependent with a specific verbal ability. And the changes take place roughly between the ages of five and eight, after considerable communicative verbal fluency in the form of the production of appropriate and grammatical sentential strings has been achieved. These studies point the way to the specific respects in which human language is very different from animal communication systems, as well as to the character of its cognitive adaptive utility.

17   Superordination

It has long been known that terms of reference, especially proper names and names for particular people, such as 'Mommy', 'Daddy', and 'Baby', are among the very first words learned by children (Anglin, 1977; cf. also Huttenlocher, 1974; Keil, 1979). Numerous studies also show that the child's early vocabulary is concrete, in some respect that is not pre-theoretically clear, compared to the vocabulary of adults: the nouns in the child's vocabulary are characteristically nouns for medium-sized physical objects and stuff: 'car', 'doggie', 'milk'; its descriptions are desciptions of properties, functions or parts that have a certain sensory immediacy: 'It barks', 'You smell flowers', 'It runs, with wheels on it', are some responses to 'What is a dog?', 'What is a flower?', 'What's a car?'. The responses have been characterized as "instance oriented" (Anglin, 1977, pp. 190–6, 229).

But the most intriguing result is Anglin's report that two- and three-year-old children, children at the earliest stage of language learning, do not exhibit any mastery of superordination in concept attainment. That is, in their answers to questions of the sort 'What is a dog/a car/cereal?' they overwhelmingly cite particular instances of these things, either multiple instances or examples of unique individuals, for example, 'Martha's dog', even though

they appear to have some knowledge of the appropriate superordinate – 'animal', 'vehicle', 'food'. Although ready to answer
the question 'What is a VW?' and 'What is a robin?' with,
respectively, 'a car' and 'a bird', they are equally ready to respond to 'What is a car?' and 'What is a bird?' with 'a VW' and
'a robin' (Anglin, 1977, p. 41; see also Brown, 1958; Anglin,
1970; Keil, 1979, p. 135). During this same period, children are
able to identify what seem to be new instances of a concept. That
is, shown a picture of a wombat, which they have never seen,
they will call it an 'animal', a picture of an old woman, 'nana'.
Nevertheless, this pre-superordinate period is marked by both
overextension and underextension of general terms (Anglin, 1977,
pp. 236ff); that is, the children characteristically apply their words
to items beyond what is included in the adult extension of the
terms and equally fail to apply the words to things to which they
do apply in adult usage. Although their overextensions have often been noted in the literature on language learning, their
underextensions have not been equally remarked, largely because
– unlike their overextensions which are marked by verbal behavior
of the wrong sort – their underextensions are often marked only
by silence in response to a query (see Milliken's discussion of this
point, 1984, and also Markman, 1989). But, Anglin points out,
the instance-orientation of their responses to the questions illustrated above, even when they know the word that is the
superordinate in adult discourse (that is, 'animal', 'vehicle', 'food'),
is itself a form of underextension.

There are different conclusions upon which one might bring
the above data to bear. Anglin used these results to provide
partial support for the hypothesis that language acquisition involves the construction by the child of a multi-modal prototype,
an internal representation of the central tendency of the instances
to which the child has been exposed which can then be used as
a guide in classifying new instances (Anglin, 1977, p. 260; and
Rosch et al., 1976). The idea is that the under- and overextensions
are evidence that the child's mental prototype is not congruent
with the adult's, and that the child's prototype is gradually
corrected until congruence is achieved. The prototype hypothesis
has been widely accepted as a replacement for the traditional
analysis of concept attainment in terms of criterial attributes

or of necessary and sufficient conditions. It has been further adapted and developed, in somewhat different services, by Hilary Putnam (1975) and Johnson-Laird (1983). Prototype-based analysis of early language learning, however, while it may be a salutary alternative to accounts based upon assumptions of criterial attributes or necessary and sufficient conditions, does not alone provide an explanation of superordinate achievement. One reason why it does not is because prototypes are, of necessity, representations of sensory aspects of things and situations; but superordinates need not be related to things or situations that have distinguishing sensory aspects, nor related to sensory aspects in a relevant way. This is not to deny that there may be prototypes for things that are abstractly characterized, such as 'Southern Senator'; but the prototype will itself have sensory aspects. However, if your understanding of human happiness is some sensory representation of a quintessentially happy prototype, you have got happiness all wrong, as the philosophers are fond of pointing out. And this, even though *assigning* a visual representation to one's goals appears to facilitate their realization. Visual representations may be strongly motivational even though they may fail to capture conceptual distinctions. And they can capture in some sense of representing conceptual distinctions without *marking* those distinctions; for example, a representation of truth consisting of a person saying "It is raining" while standing amidst drops of water must represent equally an actor on a stage or someone being tricked into a false belief by a joker who went to great lengths, and so on. Add a detail to rule out one of these and others can be summoned.

The verbal behavior described above seems to show that there is some understanding of class inclusion, since the same word is applied to several instances; yet superordination and subordination are treated as true inverses: if a robin is a bird then a bird is a robin; if a VW is a car then a car is a VW. There is, then, no clear appreciation of the hierarchical ordering of concepts/ words. 'Robin'–'bird', 'VW'–'car', 'Wheaties'–'cereal'–'food', 'Martha's dog'–'dog'–'animal': no differences of order or level are observed among these.

The developmental importance of superordinate recognition is acknowledged by Anglin:

The most dramatic advances in the child's expressible knowledge
of verbal concepts beyond this rudimentary base [that is, the names
and words for concreta mentioned above] include the ability to
assign the concept to a superordinate class and the ability to describe characteristics of instances of the concept other than the
basic concrete ones . . . which include such characteristics as the
relation of the concept to other things in the world, their internal
constituents, and their origins. (Anglin, 1977, p. 229)

Superordinate recognition seems to mark a vast change in
the child's cognitive grasp of the world, reflected by equally vast
changes in its repertoire of verbal behavior, although they are
changes that seem not to have been noticed before, perhaps because, as underextensions, they are features that were marked
more by their absence prior to superordinate recognition than
by some semantic or syntactic violation. The failure to respond
to the query 'What's cereal?' with 'food' and instead to answer
'Wheaties', even though the word 'food' is used by the child in
other contexts, is the sort of absence of a possible response that
would go unnoticed. Quite independently of the relevance of this
data to prototype theory, which itself is a major advance in
understanding the structures engaged in word-meaning, the
superordinate data raise deep questions about the character of
the child's linguistic and cognitive competencies pre- and post-
superordinate recognition. First, they raise (semantic) questions
about the interpretation of the pre-superordinate child's utterances. Does the child who says 'A bird is a robin' assert
the generic though false 'Birds are robins' in so saying? That is,
is the correct interpretation of such an utterance that the class of
birds is included in the class of robins? I think we find it most
unnatural to accept this interpretation of the child's utterance,
even though that would be the correct interpretation, albeit a
semantically anomalous as well as a false one, of the sentence in
standard grammar. We want to deny that interpretation because
the child also calls bluejays 'birds' and refuses to call them
'robins', suggesting some command of a structure of class
inclusion such that both bluejays and robins are discrete subsets
of birds. Instead, we take the child to be using a non-standard
sentential form to say something like 'A robin is something that

is called a "bird" ', having interpreted the question 'What's a bird?' to be a request for an example of a bird, a request for a name of a bird, rather than a request for a predicate that is true of birds.

18   The Cognitive Import of Superordination

These data on superordinate acquisition also raise certain cognitive questions. Is there some uniform cognitive change that takes place from pre- to post-superordinate recognition? If there is, we would expect such a difference to be reflected syntactically as well as semantically and to be subtle, although perhaps very deep. Here is a characterization of one syntactic difference between pre- and post-superordination, with samples set off in brackets. In adult English discourse, questions of the form:

   Wh– is F?

can be syntactically ambiguous. For example, the question:

   What is red?

can be interpreted either as a request to close the open sentence:

   ____ is red.   [The book is red.]

by supplying a subject, or as a request to complete the sentence:

   Red is ____.   [Red is a color.]

by supplying a predicate. Other questions of the form 'Wh– is F?' are not syntactically ambiguous in mature discourse. The question 'Who is tired?', for example, has only the first sort of syntactic interpretation, as a request to close the open sentence:

   ____ is tired.   [Daddy is tired.]

while 'What is beauty?' has only the second sort of syntactic interpretation, as a request to complete the sentence:

Beauty is ____.

by supplying a predicate such as, for example, 'only skin deep', 'in the eye of the beholder' or 'a transcendental idea'.

In mature discourse, questions of the form:

'What is an N?'

are unambiguous requests for answers of the form:

An N is a ____.

where a predicate that is superordinate to the N in the question is supplied. The pre-superordinate, however, interprets wh–questions of the form:

What is an N?   [What is a car?]

as requests to close an open sentence of the form:

____ is an N.   [A VW is a car.]

by supplying a subject. The pre-superordinate does not understand that the correct interpretation of such a question is unambiguously as a request to complete a sentence of the form:

An N is a ____.   [A car is a vehicle.]

by supplying a predicate. The pre-superordinate always interprets these questions as requests for a subject term and never as requests for a predicate term. (Anecdote: While working on this book, one Christmas I found myself in the company of a $6\frac{1}{2}$-year-old boy much taken with transportation toys. Out of curiosity I queried, "What's a vehicle?" He answered, "A car." A few minutes later, conversation about other matters between boy and parents having intervened, I asked, "What's a car?"; he scrambled through the presents littering the floor, picked up one of the toys and held it up, saying "This!") Is this merely a syntactic quirk, a bit of syntax that the child hasn't yet mastered? Or is there a semantic and cognitive dimension to this phenomenon? Here is one account of what goes on.

The child's pre-superordinate sentences are extensional. That is, the general terms in them – the categorematic terms – function as multiple names for the same thing, as the same person might be 'Mary', 'Mrs Smith', and 'Mama', or common names for different things, as each member of the Smith family is called 'Smith'. The child is, if you like, a little nominalist, treating the words and phrases, even the verbals 'pick', 'drive it', 'runs', as labels for sensory presenta. The child's struggle is to get the labels right, that is, to match the labels with what it takes to be distinguishable things in a way that is congruent with adult discourse. There are many labels, however, and even more "things"; in particular, many things that are distinguishable to the child get matched with the same label. Probably, many things that are indistinguishable to the child are given different labels.

The child guesses, with much reinforcement, the pattern of adult correlations. Success is only partial. The problem is that there is no one-to-one correlation of semantic elements of a language with items in the world that are uniformly identifiable by random members of a language community independently of and prior to the acquisition of a language. Words are not mere labels; mere names of sensory presenta. Therefore, as long as the child follows the label-matching strategy, the product is bound to exhibit mismatch with adult discourse; the mismatch manifesting itself in underextension and overextension. No doubt the construction of multi-modal prototypes improves this matching performance, considering that our sensory equipment has rather a large role to play in our discourse practices and that most early discourse situations focus on concrete and present items whose distinctness from their background is reinforced by non-verbal as well as verbal interactions and by their roles in satisfying (or failing to satisfy) the prelinguistic wants, needs, and interests of the child. Treating words and phrases as labels, very likely supplemented by prototype construction, the child goes a long way toward approximating the adult correlations. But this strategy, even when exhaustively applied, does not ultimately work; first, because, as mentioned, there is no one-to-one correlation of semantic elements of a language with items in the world that can be identified uniformly and independently of knowing the language; and, second, because prototypes themselves will suffer from the same possibilities of mismatch and are limited in their semantic usefulness to relatively concrete terms. Underextension and over-extension persist.

If this characterization of pre-superordinate discourse is roughly correct, then the 'is' of the child's 'A bird is a robin' in answer to 'What's a bird?' is not the copula of predication but must be an 'is' of equality between labels: 'robin' and 'bird' are two labels that can apply to the same thing; 'robin' is another name for a thing that 'bird' is a name for. Certainly the child is not predicating of birds that they have the property of being robins. Despite the fact that the child's discourse has the rudimentary sentence structures of subject–predicate form, the pre-superordination data together with the syntactic structure of the child's interpretation of wh– questions show that the child does not grasp the distinctive semantic roles of subjects and predicates. Set theory, perhaps even the calculus of individuals, may provide appropriate structures for modelling the extensional language of the pre-superordinate. Multi-modal prototypes, as Roger Brown (1978) has pointed out, can be treated set-theoretically. Indeed, they are like mental images (albeit unseen ones) and Lockean ideas in this respect.

The account I am proposing here is that superordinate recognition marks the acquisition of intensional linguistic-cognitive structures. With the achievement of superordination, proto-predicates, that is, expressions occupying predicate positions in the early sentences but treated as names, become genuine predicates, making possible such characteristically human cognitive activities as explicit judgments of truth and falsehood and assertion. Superordination consists in learning predicates for protopredicates; its effect is to turn those protopredicates into genuine predicates.[6] How does this process work? How does superordination result in intensionality? The results of Frank Keil's (1979) research into the acquisition of certain ontological predicates suggest how it may work.

19 The Categorial Structure of Discourse

Keil's 1979 study is concerned with the acquisition of ontological categories that are instantiated by words such as 'physical object' and 'event' rather than the more concrete categories (for example, 'robin' and 'bird') of Anglin's research. Because of their abstract character, Keil's examples seem capable of being acquired only as superordinates whereas considerable fluency with words like 'car', 'food', and 'flower' is exhibited prior to any evidence of superordinate achievement. For this reason, Keil's data may focus more directly on the developmental mechanisms of superordinate acquisition.

Keil reports that a category label or name is acquired before the child associates any predicate expression specifically with the label. Rather, the label, or category name, appears to be directly associated with items to which the child presumes that it applies; only later does the child become aware of any other predicates that are uniquely associated with the first one. Throughout this developmental period, a hierarchical progression is noted in which categories (that is, predicates or general terms) develop out of other categories, first by negation and only later by positive, higher-level predication, that is, what has here been called superordination. Keil says:

> The pattern seems to be that children become aware of a category via its terms [members] before they become aware of its unique predicates. In this progression [of acquiring higher-order categories] categories often seem to develop out of other categories. That is, children do not suddenly realize that there are physical objects, events, and abstract objects; rather, they suddenly realize that some things are not physical objects. They are not sure what these are; they just know what they are not. Moreover, younger children do not start with a syncretic concept of "physical object–abstract object–event" out of which the three separate notions emerge. Rather, they have only the concept "physical object," and everything is considered to be a physical object. When children first make the distinction, they do not have an equally clear idea of what both categories are like; on the contrary, they only know that there are some unclear things that do not fit into the

clear cases of physical objects. The same pattern is seen at other nodes. The class of abstract things seems to differentiate out of the class of events, the class of liquids out of the class of objects with boundaries, and the class of plants out of the class of animals. . . . Categories appear to develop out of other categories. (Keil, 1979, pp. 78–80)

Keil's results add confirmation to the hypothesis that a particular word is treated by the child as merely a label for one or more "things" it happens to distinguish, whatever the basis for its so distinguishing. The child first engages in simple coding, attempting to find the correlation that will be deemed acceptable by adults. There is no reason to suppose that it would ever succeed in getting the presumed correlation right by proceeding in this way. *The leap that superordinate recognition marks is the child's sudden grasp that there are labels "for" some of its labels*, that is to say, that there are predicates for predicates (that is, for its proto-predicates).[7] For example, the same items can be called 'food' and 'groceries'; they earn the label 'food' because the predicate 'edible' applies to them; they earn the label 'groceries' because the predicate 'purchased' applies to them. 'Groceries' is not just another name for what 'food' names; it is what food that is purchased is called. Words are not merely labels applied to things on the basis of their apparent sensory resemblance, with some things that exhibit such resemblance somehow nevertheless warranting different labels; some labels apply to things because other labels apply to them! Perhaps, in the child's mind at this decisive moment in its ontogenesis, some labels apply to things only because other labels apply to them. The additional sensory input that enables the child to make this leap into intensionality is simply the data that what other folks call things is sometimes itself the only basis it can use for sorting things into distinct categories; that some categories are distinguished from other categories solely by the fact that others use different labels for them. There may not be forthcoming any more "natural" data about the things so categorized except that certain labels are applied to them alone by the members of the language community; and those labels are applied to them because other labels are applied to them by the community and not because of any sensory similarity, analogy, or prototypical relations among them.

It is here, with the dawning of intensionality that is requisite for predication, that bottom-up meets top-down. The *is* of attribution, the copula, cannot be supposed part of the child's cognitive repertoire until this leap has been made. In an earlier idiom, this transition initiates judgment. Relationships among general terms, as they are applied to things by the members of the language community on the basis of other knowledge about them than what is represented in immediate perception, make the transition necessary and possible. These relationships cannot be constructed by the child alone, using physical or computational operations on anything "internal" to it. Indeed, the relationships among the labels might be contradictory, irrational, impossible. None of that matters to the task; what matters is that those relationships among the labels are entrenched in the practices of the language community. The relationships that cannot be the product of the child's isolated constructional efforts must be given to it by the community.

20 Conclusion

If the hypothesis given here for interpreting the data on superordinate acquisition is correct, then there are numerous consequences for the theory of human mentality as well as for the general theory of language. The most central of these consequences will be considered in subsequent chapters, but a glimpse can be given here.

First, it provides an explanation why language acquisition is not perspicuously conceptualized as the breaking of a code, of successfully arriving at the right correlation of semantic units of a language with items in the extralinguistic world, units and items being identifiable independently of the language. Although mature linguistic competence might be capable of being modelled by such correlational structures, a first language is the product of a process that is not fundamentally a coding process because the resulting correlations are between items that are themselves partly constructed by the essentially social process of learning the language.

Second, one assumption of the Standard Theory seems, on the above considerations, to be false. It is that propositional structures, in particular, subject–predicate structures of the form x *is* F, are given pre-linguistically. In situation semantics, this is the Realist assumption that information is prior to language (Barwise and Perry, 1983). In information-theoretic semantics (Dretske, 1981), it is the assumption that the source (s) carries information of the sort *that s is F*. In psychosemantics (Fodor, 1975), it is the assumption that when a child learns a first language it learns to pair the predicates of that language with something like a co-extensive concept, via a truth rule perhaps; for example, the predicate 'ball' and its concept, F, via the rule:

$$\langle y \text{ is a ball} \rangle \text{ is true if and only if } x \text{ is } F$$

Thus, Fodor's Language of Thought hypothesis, that the child must already have one of these concepts in order to be able to learn the language, depends essentially upon the assumption that concepts with propositional structure are part of the functioning cognitive system prior to language acquisition. However, if predication is a cognitive ability acquired during the essentially social process of language learning, then the assumption that propositional structures of subject–predicate form are pre-linguistically given is gratuitous, at best. However, since there is also no empirical evidence possible in support of that assumption, a stronger judgment is warranted.

The consequences of this hypothesis that shed the greatest light on the question of the relations between language and knowledge, however, are positive ones. For the categorial structure of language that is revealed in these studies of language acquisition promises to sustain an explanation of how humans can successfully refer to things about which they do not know everything there is to be known as well as to things that are the artifacts of their own practices. In particular, it reveals why a language is better thought of as a social institution which the child enters by leap or catapult rather than as an internal structure that is the product of purely rational or causal processes.

Both Empiricist and Nativist theories of language learning have historically sought some pre-linguistically identifiable semantic elements of a language that could be code-correlated by the language learner with language-independent, pre-linguistically identifiable elements of the world. Chapter 2 aimed to show that there are persuasive reasons for thinking that such a search and its theoretical drive are mistaken. In this chapter, an alternative to such codely conceptualizations of language acquisition is introduced, one that is suggested by recent results in developmental research. Now the burden of assessing the plausibility of this hypothesis must be undertaken.

Notes

1 *Very* roughly speaking, to say that some mental content is individualistic is to claim that a person's mental content is determined entirely and exclusively by the person's internal constitution, and not at all by any features of the external environment (but for subtle distinctions here, see Davies, 1991, p. 463). The views I end up supporting in this essay have an anti-individualist flavor, siding with Burge and Davies, but I find much of the general debate about "mental content" needlessly obscure, particularly in the manner in which minds are reified, *à la* Descartes. Hence, I have avoided entering this debate through its own portals, preferring some side doors with fewer theoretical obstructions.

2 What Stich (1983, p. 75) calls the "strong language-of-thought hypothesis" is tantamount to what I am calling a "Linguistic Supervenience Thesis".

3 The computationalist version of this supervenience thesis tries to surmount the problems of dealing with an open system – human cognitive practice – as if it were a closed one by positing different "levels of explanatory principles". Thus, Pylyshyn posits three levels: "The picture of cognitive (or "mental") processing we end up with is one in which the mind is viewed as operating upon *symbolic representations* or *codes*. The semantic content of these codes corresponds to the content of our thoughts (our beliefs, goals, and so on). Explaining cognitive behavior requires that we advert to three distinct levels of this system: the nature of the mechanism or functional architecture; the nature of the codes (that is, the symbol structures); and their semantic content" (Pylyshyn, 1984, pp. xvii–xviii). Obviously, this project requires positing primitives of some sort as code-correlata, at least in each of the higher levels; but we

have seen in chapter 2 that this presumption is mistaken in the case of linguistic cognitive functions. Chomsky (1986) proposes to avoid this objection by redefining language as what he calls "I-language" – basically, language as represented in the physical brain! One problem with this strategy is that we can know about I-language, and in principle, only from external linguistic behavior, what Chomsky calls E-language and considers of no theoretical importance. For more on this see note 5 below.

4   I suppose the suppressed premise leading from the innateness of the LAD to the uniqueness of the grammar is an assumption that there is a uniquely correct description of any physical structure, although I am not aware of any place in the relevant literature where this premise is explicit. This premise is, of course, highly dubious. The metaphor of "hard-wiring" may contribute to its attractiveness (a wire is either *there* or it *isn't*).

5   The conclusion that study of language acquisition, and diachronic linguistic study in general, is not a source of data for a theory or model of linguistic competence or of the nature of the language faculty has remained unchanged in Chomsky's work since its early (1965) statement to the present, although the argument given to support it has altered. In *Knowledge of Language* (1986) a distinction is made between E-language, "language regarded as an externalized object," and I-language, "the system of [linguistic] knowledge attained and internally represented in the mind/brain" (p. 24). E-language "appears to play no role in the theory of language" (p. 26) because "The language faculty is a distinct system of the mind/brain, with an initial state S^0 common to the species . . . and apparently unique to it in essential respects. Given appropriate experience, this faculty passes from the state S^0 to some relatively stable steady state S^s, which then undergoes only peripheral modification" (p. 25). "[T]he concept of E-language, however construed, appears to have no significance" (p. 31).

6   I take it that Vygotsky is describing exactly this transition, but more creatively, in this passage from *Mind in Society* (1978, p. 98): "As I discussed in earlier chapters, a special feature of human perception (one arriving at a very early age) is the so-called perception of real objects, that is, the perception of not only colors and shapes, but also meaning. Humans do not merely see something round and black with two hands; they see a clock and can distinguish one thing from another. Thus, the structure of human perception could be figuratively expressed as a ratio in which the object is the numerator and the meaning is the denominator (object/meaning). This ratio

symbolizes the idea that all human perception is made up of generalized rather than isolated perceptions. For the child the object dominates in the object/meaning ratio and meaning is subordinated to it. At the initial moment when a stick becomes the pivot for detaching the meaning of *horse* from a real horse, this ratio is inverted and meaning predominates, giving meaning/object."

7 The phrases "labels for ... its labels" and "predicates for predicates" are used here in order to capture, concisely, the anomalousness of the child's semantic-syntactic grasp at this crucial point: in addition to matching expressions with items and scenes, the child must match, so to speak, expressions with expressions. But this characterization, it will later emerge, grossly oversimplifies both the child's semantic situation and the child's problematic.

4 Society in Mind

Now language was first the attitude, glance of the eye, movement of the body and its parts indicating the oncoming social act to which the other individuals must adjust their conduct. It becomes language in the narrower sense when through his gesture the individual addresses himself as well as the others who are involved in the act. His speech is their speech. He can address himself in their gestures and thus present to himself the whole social situation within which he is involved, so that not only is conduct social but consciousness becomes social as well.

G. H. Mead, "The Psychology of Punitive Justice"

21 The Superordination Hypothesis

The hypothesis that genuine predication does not occur in the utterances of the language learner until superordination is achieved, I shall call the Superordination Hypothesis. There are, to be sure, many problems both in stating the hypothesis and in understanding what its claim amounts to. The hypothesis nevertheless identifies a locus and a route through which a society's conceptualization of phenomena enters an individual's psyche. It is also a wedge into a host of otherwise puzzling phenomena, linguistic and cognitive, about which there are many models for mature discourse but models that are opaque to language learning. This last is, in part, why Nativist accounts of language learning are so appealing: what such accounts describe as mature competence (cf. chapter 2) could not be otherwise explained than as issuing directly from preexisting inborn structures, including preexisting concepts. There is no conceivable way by which such a code correlation could be learned, particularly if what is meant by *to learn* is to be produced directly by the individual learner exclusively out of raw non-linguistic empirical input to the physical system together with the sound patterns of the language to which the learner is exposed (section 13). The alternative proposed here begins with a different conception of what is achieved in attaining linguistic competence: Initial language entry marks the onset of conceptualization.[1]

The Superordination Hypothesis also suggests a path, between those two opposed cul-de-sacs, from which to approach the problem of "the emergence of logical resources". Macnamara, after rejecting the Nativist view that imputes beliefs to infants, says, "I am even more uncomfortable with the idea that we can derive logical resources from the performance of logic-free operations" (1986, p. 29), a position he attributes to Quine, Piaget, and, more tentatively, to Wittgenstein.[2] From the present perspective, Macnamara is right to reject both alternatives, although the course he adopts seems equally problematic. Macnamara's solution is to impute a concept of truth and a few related logical concepts, but *not* the capacity for propositional thought, to the pre-logical infant. He thus follows a limited version of the nativist hypothesis. In his focus on logic acquisition instead of language acquisition, however, Macnamara commits Piaget's errors of (1) ignoring the role that articulate language appears to play in the growth of reasoning, and (2) supposing that currently entrenched theories of logic provide optimal and unique descriptions of mental operations that are universal among humans – that is, that they are empirical theories, *and* correct ones. But a more serious problem is to understand how one could have *concepts* of truth (truth of what?), contradiction, and negation prior to having a capacity to entertain propositions.

21.1 Intrinsic and Extrinsic Representations

A tangle of problems seems to curse efforts to describe the infant's psychology, a tangle even more dense than that met in trying to describe an adult's consciousness. Some help through the thicket is provided by Stephen Palmer's (1978) work on representation theory. In developing his theory, Palmer is concerned to sharpen the issues between those who claim that "mental representation is" propositional and those who claim that "it" has an analog structure (p. 294). It is the conceptual distinctions Palmer introduces between different types of representation that are of interest here, but it is worth an interruption to take note first of his conclusion concerning the propositional/analog debate, and of a recent research result that has equally close bearing on the Superordination Hypothesis.

Palmer's conclusion is that the two types of representation, propositional and analog, are informationally equivalent as representations and, for this reason, he believes the controversy could not be resolved without physiological psychologists "looking inside the head" (p. 298). Palmer claims that manifested behavior reveals only what information a subject has and does not reveal the form in which the information is stored; while the difference between an analog and a propositional representation is in the inherent structure of the representation. More recently, however, Hart and Gordon (1992) report behavioral research results with a neurologically impaired subject which, they maintain, "mandate the existence of two distinct representations" of the physical attributes of animals "in normal individuals, one visually based and one language-based" (p. 60). These results are also said to "establish that knowledge of physical attributes is strictly segregated" in the language system from knowledge of other properties.[3] In Palmer's terms, their claim is to have acquired behavioral evidence that establishes the existence of a (visual) analog representational system distinct from a (linguistic) propositional representational system. That the linguistic representation should be distinct from the visual representation is, *prima facie*, a result to be expected if the Superordination Hypothesis is correct, for the hypothesis says, in effect, that linguistic meaning is an achievement by the child of a new cognitive ability that is distinct from whatever earlier (active) cognitive capacities the pre-linguistic infant instantiates.

Palmer also concludes that cognitive psychology is concerned only with matters at "the level of abstraction defined by informationally equivalent systems" (1978, p. 277) which could effectively, although it seems indefensible, exclude the Superordination Hypothesis from the domain of cognitive psychology.

Palmer distinguishes between analog and propositional representations according to whether a representation is related to what it represents in virtue of relations intrinsic to the representation or in virtue of an extrinsic relation to that which it represents. For example, to represent the distribution of ages in a population by rectangular columns of different heights would be to use an intrinsic representation, since the columns represent ages by virtue of the relations of column heights to one another, one that inheres in the representation. The inherent structural characteristics of the representation constrain what it can function as a representation for. A proposition, on the other hand, is said, on this scheme, to represent something only by virtue of a relation to something external to it – that for which it is a true description.[4] So, Palmer calls propositions "extrinsic" representations, because they are constrained in what they can represent by their relation to something external to them.

Although there are complicated problems for this characterization of the difference between analog and propositional representations, the difference between intrinsic and extrinsic relations in virtue of which one thing may represent another may be useful in describing more sharply the content of the Superordinate Hypothesis. The hypothesis is that the achievement of superordination marks the beginning of availability to the child of an extrinsic representational system that is distinct from the child's earlier, intrinsic representational systems.

There is another dimension of usefulness to Palmer's distinctions. When theorists describe the infant as having beliefs, or concepts of truth, negation, and contradiction, probably they do not mean thereby to be attributing an extrinsic representational system, available for use, to the child. Perhaps they mean only to refer to uses of the child's intrinsic representational systems that have some analogy with uses of the extrinsic system that subtends propositional thought. It is clear that those intrinsic representational "systems" are preconditions to superordination.

21.2   Language Entry

A leap into language occurs with superordinate recognition. I use "leap" here, first, to indicate that language entry is not effected either by deductive or physico-causal processes that are wholly internal to the language learner, and not that such entry is mysterious or inexplicable. Indeed, it is a major aim of this essay to suggest a cogent and empirically adequate explanation of the conditions which facilitate the relevant cognitive transition in the child. "Facilitate" rather than yield this transition, both because conditions in the natural world never guarantee results (they are always dependent for their efficacy upon the initial state of the organism and environment) and because not all children do in fact enter the language. Indeed, if the account developed here is correct to some degree, it may provide the basis for an explanation of one type of childhood autism: failure to make this leap into semantic intensionality.

There is another reason why "leap" engages an appropriate metaphor. The account to be proposed will postulate at least two stages of development, each of which is essentially contingent upon the linguistic practices of the language community; neither stage is a result of mechanical processes or procedures wholly internal to the language initiate.

The notion of language entry, on the other hand, is not intended as a metaphor. It refers, rather, to one dynamic relation which an individual may bear to a social practice, social object, or other artifact. Just as one becomes a member of some organization by joining or being inducted into it, and one enters into or executes a contract with others, the relation between a language intitiate and the linguistic practices of the community is one of entering into a communal practice. None of these relations is a metaphor for something else which is better or more literally described in some other way.[5]

With this leap the language learner enters, at some location, a social institution that contains, in practice, nested hierarchies of predicates. The learner enters into an interpersonal and cooperative practice that depends essentially upon the presumption of that hierarchy; that is, the practice assumes the hierarchy and this assumption is necessary for the practice to continue and to be passed on to the novice. Failure to grasp what Strawson (1971) has called "the asymmetry of subjects and predicates" explains the persisting underextension and overextension of the pre-superordinate's usage. Entry into the language is marked by a major shift forward in approximating adult usage, and this shift is accomplished through superordinate achievement.

21.3 Genetic Fallacies

Although the wedge that this hypothesis creates has a wide nether end, its thin end invites many questions. Not the least of them is why any facts about language learning should be relevant to understanding the nature of the product of that learning, that is, language competence or the social institution that is a language. Isn't it a fallacy to suppose that the origin of something sheds light upon its nature? The answer to this question is "Yes and no", depending upon what one means by 'fallacy'. If one thinks of formal fallacies, then one might suppose that unless the origins of everything *entail* conclusions about their natures, then it is a fallacy to think that from the origins of anything one can conclude something about its nature; that this is what it is to be a fallacy. One might however, and I think more appropriately, think of the "informal" fallacies as rather providing guidelines about generalizations to avoid for the most part, since the selected character of their premises (here, being about origins) does not *guarantee* the truth of their conclusions (about natures). Generally, for instance, the origin of a belief has no bearing on the truth of the belief: one can come to believe that Wren designed the Sheldonian through reliable or unreliable routes. Which sort of route it was is irrelevant to the truth of that belief: the belief can be true or false, regardless of someone's route to that belief. However, sometimes the origin of a belief *has bearing* on its truth, for some routes relative to some beliefs are more reliable indicators of the belief's truth than others. So, if extensive archaeological research leads one to believe that the Druids engaged in ritual sacrifice then one has followed a route that is more reliable relative to that belief than would be, say, consulting a novel about Druids, even though the novel might provide evidence concerning what beliefs about Druids are currently popular.

I am suggesting that data about language learning are relevant to understanding the nature of mature linguistic competence in contrast with views according to which they are not relevant.[6] There are two major reasons why facts about language learning are relevant to a theory of language. One is that, despite the inherently social character of language, language is also a natural phenomenon and the origins of natural phenomena are relevant to understanding them, their internal composition and structures and their relations to other things. How the DNA molecule gets built is good evidence – perhaps the best – that it has a particular structure and functions in a certain way. Note that the relation between the origin of a natural phenomenon and its functioning is often, however, only evidential rather than necessitating. This is because a product can have properties that are not explicable purely in terms of its generating "cause" (section 13); it can acquire such properties as a result of relations it has to other things external to its originating cause. Properties acquired in this way can, in turn, contravene properties the subject would otherwise have had merely as a result of its internal history. Thus the fact that drivers of motor vehicles are legally responsible for their actions is a property that contravenes (by superseding) many properties which normal drivers would otherwise have as a result of their internal physical history, to the extent that ignorance of the relevant laws – if knowledge and ignorance were understood, *per impossibile*, as internally determined properties of a subject – will not excuse a violation. The innocence that ignorance normally effects is here contravened by the external conditions of legislation.

A second reason why facts about language learning are relevant to a general theory of language is that they are the closest we can come to understanding what changes having a language makes to our cognitive life. Once we have a language, we cannot in the normal course of events do anything that would constitute introspecting our own mental lives *sans* language, and so we cannot by introspection compare consciousness with and without language, thereby to learn what difference a language makes. (Perhaps there is in this something of relevance to the interpretation of transcendental phenomenology.) Nor is it empirically acceptable to try to remember what our conscious lives were like before we had language, for either our predilection for the fallacy of hindsight in its most poignant form (see William James on Mr Ballard and Wittgenstein's commentary on this report in his *Investigations*) endows all our childhood memories with verbal forms *ex post facto*, or else we have virtually no explicitly recallable memories prior to functioning language. If, then, we expect a theory of language to accommodate an explanation of the cognitive advantages with which language endows humans, we must attend to facts about language acquisition in such theorizing. Syntactic and semantic theories according to which the pre-linguistic child, and perhaps members of other species, can entertain propositions have abstracted their domains of inquiry from the empirical data too soon.[7]

22   Unavailable Routes to Language Entry

Among the consequences of this hypothesis for theories of mind and language, a foremost one is that a child's entry into a language cannot be either by purely rational procedures or by purely physico-causal processes.

First, entry into a first language cannot be by rational procedures, either of deduction or of formulating hypotheses.[8] If, prior to superordination, the child does not have functioning predication, then, first of all, the child cannot perform normal logical operations with or on standard subject–predicate propositions, neither operations of categorical syllogistic nor of the predicate calculus, since to do so would require awareness of the functional differences between subjects and predicates – quite independently of questions about quantification. But there is a second type of case to consider. For, even though the pre-superordinate is admitted not to have functional grasp of subject–predicate structures, perhaps it might entertain propositions that are *not* of subject–predicate form, such as *It's raining* or *Mary is taller than*

John.[9] Could the pre-superordinate enter its language by performing deductions using a sentential calculus with, or by hypothesizing about, sentences that do not have subject – predicate form? The right answer seems to be that if the child does not have genuine predication, then among the predicates that it doesn't have is the predicate 'is true'. Excluding the problematic realm of the assertions of pure mathematics, there seems to be no way by which a person without either that predicate or one that is functionally equivalent to it can perform logical operations on or with assertions in a natural language. This is not to say that one could not learn to play computational games, perhaps even in accordance with rules that exhibit some isomorphism to deductive or hypothetical structures, or to the grammar of some language, without such a predicate. But one cannot perform substantive deductions or inductions, so as to arrive thereby at a proposition as a genuine conclusion about some subject, and know that it is about that subject, without such a predicate. In fact, it is difficult to see how one who has no concept of truth can *entertain any propositions*, and this quite independently of the question whether any propositions are known to be true.[10] An epistemological position of extreme skepticism about the possibility of knowledge of truths and a metaphysical position of relativism – that there are no absolutely true propositions but only ones that are true relative to some perspective or other – are compatible both with having a truth predicate and with being able to perform logical operations with propositions. Logic doesn't depend upon there being any true propositions, but only upon the possibility of assuming some propositions to be true.[11]

Another way of approaching the above relations is to see that the predicate *is true* is itself a superordinate. What it is superordinate to is *proposition* (or *statement, sentence,* or *assertion*). But *proposition* (and its companions) is a general term; *is a proposition*, a predicate. What enables us to identify the category of propositions (things to which that predicate correctly applies) seems to be our entrenched use of the predicate *is true*. If what enables us to identify a category, to "have a concept", is our coming to learn its entrenched superordinates, then if one doesn't have any of the relevant superordinates one cannot have a conception of the things that it superordinates, that is, of its subordinates. Knowing what a term means in a language requires knowing superordinates for the term, and in a case such as this one where all the terms, superordinates and subordinates, are abstract ones, knowing relevant superordinates may well be virtually all that there *is* to knowing what the term means. A child who does not yet have superordination cannot have a truth predicate and cannot, therefore, entertain propositions since to "entertain a proposition" is to entertain that it is or could be true. It follows that such a child cannot enter a language by means of a deductive or inductive procedure.

I acknowledge that this argument contains a number of contentions that are currently subject to debate, for example that first-order logic does not provide a complete description of the structure of any possible human language. This contention, however, is one of the central theses that this essay aims to support, by both empirical and conceptual argument; it is thus not a thesis that can be established by one argument.[12] The above argument also runs against some working assumptions of empirical research in developmental cognitive psychology that will be discussed shortly.

That a child cannot enter a language purely by means of a physical, causal process is a consequence of the considerations raised in the preceding chapter concerning the non-supervenience, in any interesting or revealing way, of superordinate achievement upon physical processes internal to the language learner, or even upon these together with purely physical input from the environment. Superordinate achievement does not supervene upon these because it involves, in an essential way, the entrenched predication *practices* of the members of the language community, practices which are no more equivalent to physical stimuli than are motor vehicle laws. Indeed, to characterize something as a "practice" is tantamount to projecting some physical stimuli in a certain direction. The child must eventually notice and take a certain auditory string produced by a member of its language community to be itself the distinguishing feature of what had previously seemed undistinguished to the child. But the child cannot literally hypothesize, propositionally, this solution. Nothing else has worked;

frustration and puzzlement loom. And then, Eureka! And it works. What works? Taking second-order predicates, whose linguistic meaning is not yet known to the child and so that have not previously functioned as predicates for the child, as distinguishers. Thus, two things (stimuli or items) that are themselves undistinguished for the child are recognized by the child as distinguishable by means of and in virtue of the differences in the "predicates" applied to them by the adult linguistic community.

23   Two Questions

There are numerous details concerning the content of the proposed hypothesis that require attention. In particular, two related questions need to be acknowledged, although only the first of them will be directly attended to now. That is the question how, on this hypothesis, we are to interpret pre-superordinate speech. More specifically, what cognitive abilities does it manifest? The remarks made so far about this topic, although they are suggestive, are still only remarks. What is needed is a more detailed account of the differences between the linguistic and cognitive characters of pre- and post-superordinate speech. But, second, if superordinate achievement is tantamount to the initiation of a higher-order cognitive ability called, perhaps, "predication", then what is predication? Neither question is simple and the two are interrelated. For to claim that prior to superordinate achievement there is no genuine predication in the child's speech is to constrain what is to count as predication as well as how pre-superordinate child speech is to be construed. The two questions differ, however, in the dangers they pose. Whereas the first question invites an excursion into speculative psychology, the second invokes entrenched problems in the philosophy of logic that are historically inimical to psychological considerations. Neither excursion sounds prudent. But if the hypothesis is correct, then both questions need to be broached. I turn now to the question how early, pre-superordinate speech might be construed, saving until the next chapter separate consideration of the question what predication is.

24 Interpreting Early Speech

Between the ages of three and five there is considerable verbal activity and of a complicated sort. Prior to superordinate acquisition, whole grammatical sentences are formed. In Anglin's (1977) studies, standard answers to questions of the sort 'What is a flower?' included not only 'A tulip' but also 'They're round' and 'You smell flowers.' These competencies prior to superordinate recognition present problems for the proposed hypothesis. What are we to make of them? In particular, if a child answers the question 'What is a dog?' with 'They bark' and the question 'What's a car?' with 'It runs, with wheels on it' or 'It's something that has a steering wheel', why should it be denied that the child is engaged in predication, predicating barking of dogs and having steering wheels of cars? The Standard Theory described in chapter 1 gives exactly this answer.

24.1 Infant Theoreticians

One of the most productive research paradigms for investigating infant cognitive resources since Roger Brown's classic *A First Language* (1973) has been the conception of the infant as entertaining hypotheses and theories to explain the events of which it is thought to be aware. Changes exhibited in the infant's behavior, from its achievement of syntactic skills to its improved understanding of the mental lives of others, have been attributed within this paradigm to the infant's correction and replacement of faulty hypotheses and theories with ones more closely resembling the way things are in the real world (or the way we adults think they are). This paradigm has enabled researchers to avoid some of the morasses of metaphysics, cosmology, and philosophical psychology into which efforts to understand human language have fallen since Plato. It has enabled researchers to acknowledge that the infant has not merely a behavioral repertoire but also a conscious life by providing a framework for describing the infant's overt behavior as exhibiting psychological content. In this way, the new paradigm has encouraged the construction of experimental designs that allow genuine research to be conducted within the difficult domain of child cognition, with a wealth of positive results.

Despite the fact that this research paradigm had its early origin in some of the assumptions of the Standard Theory that I have questioned, there are two noteworthy features of the Infant Theoretician research paradigm. First, it has provided an alternative to the classical but flawed notion that learning a concept is learning a set of essential properties which the concept defines or denotes. Second, it has provided a working solution to the deepest obstacle to empirically satisfactory research on early conceptual development: how to describe the infant's psychological content through its developmental changes without merely projecting our adult conscious contents onto them (that is, the Ballard-James Problem). That working solution, first proposed in the landmark work by Susan Carey, *Conceptual Change in Childhood* (1985), is that we conceive of children's conceptual change as analogous to theory change in adults' conceptualization of some domain.

It is important to consider, if only briefly here, what bearing the current hypothesis has on this experimentally rich and widely adopted research paradigm. The answer to this question is not transparent. A foremost consideration is that the paradigm is normally employed in describing changes from one conceptualization of a phenomenon to another, rather than in describing any initiation of conceptualization. Such changes, Carey argues, can sometimes profitably be construed as changes in theory-like conceptual structures, where differences between cognitive structures that are and those that are not theory-like is one of degree (Carey, 1985, p. 201). The current proposal certainly has no negative bearing on this suggestion. But it cannot be denied that some researchers, including Carey, think it plausible to suppose that human infants have some such conceptual structures to begin with, in, as it were, their initial state; in particular, that they have a naive mechanics and a naive (or "folk") psychology (Carey, 1985, p. 201; see also Gopnik and Wellman, 1992). However, the question whether something that should be called "conceptualization" begins at some point in a human's development or whether humans conceptualize from their "initial state", does not seem to be a clear empirical question at this stage in our understanding of these matters.[13] It is my hope that the considerations of this chapter and the next will provide some philosophical grounds for moving that question closer to the empirical realms.

However, it should be noted that I do not propose here to conduct deductive psychology, drawing, as it were, consequences about the character of early speech from the hypothesis alone that I have proposed, although this attitude has distinguished precedent. Fortunately, this is not necessary because the hypothesis itself coheres with numerous observations that have been made about early child language. In particular, theoretical efforts and experimental results in cognitive psychology provide many suggestions towards understanding pre-superordinate speech. In addition, the hypothesis may itself shed some light on and add precision to several puzzling and sometimes vague observations about the development of linguistic and cognitive competencies by the child.

24.2   Vygotsky's Proposals

For more than 20 years there has been a vast amount of research into children's acquisition of a first language, although it has not resulted in any widely accepted single theory of this phenomenon. There can be no doubt that some of this activity is attributable to the translation into English and posthumous publication of L. S. Vygotsky's informal narratives based upon his experiments on and describing the character of child language and thought (Vygotsky, 1962). Historically, it is in the research of Vygotsky that the effort to account for language learning as a socially contingent but cognitively effective process has been most fully developed. Vygotsky construes language learning as bringing about the development of new cognitive structures in the child's thought. Several of his results are relevant to the superordination hypothesis. There are also problems with his results. I shall first describe his project in general and then in greater detail before turning to these problems.

The Russian psychologist, working early in this century, called attention to the holistic character of the thought that is evident in the child's earliest uses of words and described this early phase as one in which a word functions for the child in a way similar to the way in which a proper name of an individual object functions for an adult, but initially with no stability over time in the application of the name to any same object. Subsequently, according to Vygotsky, the child makes numerous incremental transitions from this phase to one in which the word "becomes the family name of a group of objects related to one another in many kinds of ways, just as the relationships in human families are many and different" (Vygotsky, 1962, p. 62). Ultimately, the child progresses through such changing phases and stages until a plateau of mature language is reached, according to Vygotsky, in late adolescence with the attainment of conceptualization, which Vygotsky construes as resulting in speech that is based upon an analytic understanding of necessary and sufficient conditions – his essentialist understanding of word meaning. While he may have been right about the time of onset of essentialist beliefs, his understanding of conceptualization as coinciding with that onset cannot be accepted.

Of particular relevance to the Superordination Hypothesis is Vygotsky's proposal that between the ages of five and seven years categories implicit in the child's use of words change from being tied to concrete instances of the word to being applied to things on the basis of more general principles. He associated this shift with an internalization of language during this period of development, for he believed that the internalization of language provided the child with the ability to form more general and principled representations of things than memories of particular instances. Since these shifts in the child's practices of cognitive categorization were associated by Vygotsky with an internalization of language which he supposed to take place at a relatively specific time for all children, the shifts were supposed by him to take place at roughly the same time for all the child's categories. This supposition of Vygotsky's accords with the hypothesis that genuine predication enters the child's cognitive repertoire at roughly that time. The more general and principled representations would seem, in fact, not merely to be made possible by the internalization of language but actually to be a partial function of that internalization. While consensus on the theoretical side of first language acquisition appears slim, there has emerged a body of evidence that bears out many of Vygotsky's characterizations and that also provides extrinsic support for the hypothesis proposed here.

Unlike Piaget's studies, which were concerned principally with the development not of language but of the understanding of logical properties and relations, Vygotsky's experiments focused upon the development of specifically verbal thinking, what we might call discursive thought, and the role of language development in changes in the character of such thought. There are two major theses for which his work has been noted. The first is that there is thought without language; the second is that the role of words in the mental life of the developing child is radically different from their role in the adult's mental life. It often goes unnoticed, however, that he also claims that the human sort of thought, "rational" thought, is dependent upon learning the public language. In particular, Vygotsky claims that learning the public language (what Chomsky, 1986, has called "the E-language") through a long and complex process of developmental changes, makes possible and is in fact necessary to achieve true concept formation and, subsequently, the higher intellectual functions of which our species is capable (functions which his account, as noted, estimates as incomplete until late adolescence).

> The development of the processes which eventually result in concept formation begins in earliest childhood, but the intellectual functions that in specific combination form the psychological basis of the process of concept formation ripen, take shape, and develop only at puberty. . . . Learning to direct one's own mental processes with the aid of words or signs is an integral part of the process of concept formation. (Vygotsky, 1962, pp. 58-9)

The intellectual autonomy that is here described as "learning to direct one's own mental processes" cannot develop until the internalization of external speech and, with this, what Vygotsky claims is fundamental to mature internalized language, its predicative character. The phenomenal mark of what James called the "stream of thought" is predication (Vygotsky, 1962, p. 139). Those aspects of his research that bear directly on our concerns here, however, are Vygotsky's results about the child's initial learning of the public language.

24.2.1   *Phases and Bases of Conceptual Development*

Vygotsky marks numerous distinctions among the phases and stages of language acquisition in early to mid-childhood, explaining by examples and generalizations the gradations of changes in what words mean to the developing child and the varied shifting bases that the child uses in applying words to things. His most general characterization is of a gradual shift from a holistic use of words in earliest childhood to an analytic use in mid-childhood (Vygotsky, 1962, p. 76). In between these two extremes he discerns numerous changes in the bases used by the child in applying words to things. Vygotsky's experiments, it should be noted, were "pre-ethological", assigning nonsense words to simple properties of colored blocks and setting children the task of learning the meanings of these nonce words by grouping together the "right" objects – those which exemplify the meaning assigned to the nonce word by the experimenter. While his experimental design (nonsense words and laboratory setting) has been widely questioned, what is of interest here are his hypotheses. The three major phases of development of verbal concepts, the general basis for each phase and the stages within each phase that are hypothesized by Vygotsky are shown in the following chart.

Vygotsky's Developmental Phases

Phase 1:   Syncretic Image
Basis: "Heap"   –   objects are united by some subjective chance impression;
– no objective order to their union;
– highly unstable.

Stages of changing basis:
(1)   trial and error – random basis for grouping;
(2)   spatial position of the test objects – syncretic organization of the visual field;

(3) more complex base – composed of elements taken from heaps already formed by the child.

Phase 2: Thinking in Complexes
Basis: Objects are united by real bonds

Stages of changing basis:

(1) associative – based on any similarities that strike the child – a family name;
(2) collection complex – association by contrast;
(3) chain complex – family resemblance – no shared attribute as nucleus;
(4) diffuse complex – the unifying attribute keeps changing as attention shifts;
(5) the pseudo-concept – an associative complex linked by a perceptual bond – same results as classification by a shared property, but different psychological process.

Phase 3: Analytic
Basis: Objects are united by shared attributes

Stages of changing basis:

(1) grouped by maximum similarity – shared groups of attributes;
(2) grouped by a single attribute.

Some general remarks indicating, roughly, the highlights of this classification are in order. In the first, syncretic, phase, a word or sound is used in a way that is similar to the adult use of proper names; that is, there is no semantic content in the sense that an observer can notice no feature of any object that is being picked out by the child's use of the same sound and the same "word" is applied to different things on different occasions. The second phase is marked by uses of the same sound that are like the uses of a family name for a group of objects, rather than of a proper name for an individual object, and on the basis of "objective" properties of the objects; that is, properties that an observer can correlate with the child's utterance. It begins with a stage in which there is no discernible uniformity in the properties used as the basis for grouping, continues through stages that include grouping by contrasting and complementary properties (as a cup, saucer and plate might form a natural grouping), the family-resemblance basis that Vygotsky calls a "chain-complex" and, finally, to the stage of "pseudo-concepts", the stage he attributes to pre-school uses of the same word and which he believes should be called "pre-concepts" (Vygotsky, 1962, p. 90). At this pseudo-concept stage, phase 2, stage (5), the child's groupings under the same label may coincide with the adult's, but Vygotsky believes the evidence shows that a different mental operation than adult categorization is in effect. He gives the example of a child being shown a yellow triangle as the sample object. The child may pick out all the triangles in the experimental material and, so, could have been guided by the abstract concept of a triangle, but the experimental analysis shows that "in reality the child is guided by the concrete, visible likeness and has formed only an associative complex limited to a certain kind of perceptual bond. Although the results are identical, the process by which they are reached is not at all the same as in conceptual thinking" (Vygotsky, 1962, pp. 66–7).

The different processes hypothesized for phase 2, stage (5) and for phase 3 are revealed in tests where an "error" in categorizing has occurred; that is, in which the subject has not formed a group according to the meaning assigned by the experimenter to the target "word" but has included objects in its grouping that do not belong, according to the experimenter's assignment of semantic content to the nonce word. The experimenter will show the subject that one of the items has a different name on its underside from that on the sample object. Subjects who have been categorizing on the basis of the abstract concept assigned to the test name will immediately indicate that they realize they have guessed the wrong property by destroying their first grouping to start over, looking for another basis for categorizing ("'Aha! Then it is not color' [or shape, etc.]", Vygotsky quotes E. Hanfmann and J. Kasanin, 1942, pp. 30–1). Children operating with pseudo-concepts, however, instead simply remove the object that has been shown to bear the wrong name and still affirm that all the other objects belong together because, for example, they are all red. Some perceptual resemblance, rather than the abstract concept that is the assigned meaning of the word, has formed the basis for the grouping.

On the Superordination Hypothesis, the stage of pseudo-concepts belongs to the pre-superordinate stage, a stage prior to the achievement of predication. On this interpretation, the pseudo-concept behavior shows that the child has not assigned a meaning (a predicate) to the test nonsense word; the child does not realize that, using Vygotsky's example, 'mur' is to be applied to something only if 'red' applies to it; does not realize that there is a predetermined property that is the meaning of the word and which the child's grouping must exhibit. The child's grouping may in fact exhibit that property, as in the example of triangles, but this is because, as if by chance, the child has hit upon a perceptual basis for grouping that can have results that are congruent with the results of the intended conceptual basis.[14] Of course, it is not really by chance that there is a relation between some of our abstract concepts and the way things that fall under them look; for example, our Euclidian concept of a triangle and the way triangles look. Indeed, what Rosch has demonstrated to be basic categories are likely those linguistic categories (that is, predicates) which exhibit a high degree of such congruence with perceptual categories. It is also reasonable to suppose that language entry, for humans, is mediated and made possible by basic categories with just such a high degree of congruence between their perceptual and conceptual content. These last topics will be considered in greater detail in the next chapter.

Vygotsky treats phase 3, his "Analytic" phase, as developing temporally alongside phases 1 and 2 rather than as a culmination of these. And he concludes that even stage (2) of phase 3 – the child's grouping on the basis of a single attribute – need not represent the achievement of a verbal concept (a "linguistic semantic category" or a "predicate").

A concept emerges only when the abstracted traits are synthesized anew and the resulting abstract synthesis becomes the main instrument of thought. . . . Potential concepts result from a species of isolating abstraction of such a primitive nature that it is present to some degree not only in very young children but even in animals.

Hens can be trained to respond to one distinct attribute in different objects, such as color or shape, if it indicates accessible
food. (Vygotsky, 1962, pp. 78, 77)

Throughout his narrative, Vygotsky emphasizes that it is not
so much the results of the groupings as the psychological processes used to arrive at them which mark the difference between
verbal concepts (semantic categories) and non-verbal bases for
grouping different individuals together, yet appreciation of this
difference is not widely found in the literature.[15]

24.2.2 Problems of Interpretation

Vygotsky's reports are descriptively informal and creative; it is
inevitable that they admit variations in interpretation and that
they may be genuinely ambiguous. This fact is of some relevance
in determining what support his work provides for the Superordination Hypothesis as well as whether subsequent research
corroborates his claims.

As an example, consider Vygotsky's description of a contrast
between the early use of a word in a way analogous to an adult's
use of a proper name to refer to an integral whole and the later
use of a word as a family name for a group of objects related to
one another as members of a family are related to one another
(section 24.2). Both these characterizations can be understood as
describing substages of pre-superordinate speech, since the key
notion in both descriptions is that words are functioning as names
rather than as predicates or general terms.[16] Alternatively, however, the second description could be interpreted as characterizing *post*-superordinate word-meaning, in which the same word is
applied to many things in virtue of different but related features
that they have, which features are associated by the child with a
general term or phrase, a genuine predicate. The ambiguity is
between these two interpretations of the distinction:

(1)   Stage 1: words applied to things as proper names;
      Stage 2: words applied to things as shared or family names.
(2)   Stage 1: words applied to things as names;
      Stage 2: words applied to things on the basis of what

predicates are associated with the things (and with
the words).

The second interpretation would correspond roughly to the distinction implicit in the interpretation of the cognitive significance
of superordinate achievement that was suggested in chapter 3. A
review of the finer texture of Vygotsky's analysis, however, reveals no clear unique mapping of superordinate attainment into
his developmental stages in either of these ways. While both
stages of Vygotsky's third, Analytic, phase seem clearly to characterize cognitive skills that constitute what I have been calling
"predication", and while the last, pseudo-concept, stage of phase
2 does not, it is not so clear that all of the earlier stages of phase
2 are pre-superordinate stages. This unclear mapping is largely
attributable to Vygotsky's conviction that true conceptualization
is essentialist (see section 25, below).

Such problems of interpretation plague current efforts to test
further Vygotsky's conjectures and results. F. C. Keil and M. H.
Kelley (1987) review results of contemporary efforts to shed experimental light on the observations of Vygotsky and others that
children's categories shift from ones that are instance-bound to
ones that are more principled. Keil and Kelley report, however,
that "there is increasing evidence suggesting that the shift does
not occur in its entirety at a particular moment in development"
(Keil and Kelley, 1987, p. 493), as Vygotsky had hypothesized.
Instead, they claim, the evidence is that the times of such shifts
vary with different domains of discourse. However, it is not clear
that the research which they review and from which they arrive
at this conclusion is research into the *same* shift as Vygotsky's
"instance-bound to principled" shift. We have seen above that
Vygotsky proposed that there are roughly three phases of developmental change associated with different bases for using words
and that each basis admits of different stages which he characterized. Keil and Kelley review research results concerning a shift in
early usage from applying a word on the basis of characteristic
or typical features of things of that kind to applying it on the
basis of defining or essential features of things of that kind; *prima
facie*, this distinction would seem to be the distinction in changing bases that falls within phase 3, Vygotsky's "Analytic Phase",

wherein a shift occurs from applying a word on the basis of maximal similarity of attributes to applying it on the basis of a single "essential" attribute. But Keil and Kelley consider the shift from characteristic to defining feature bases to be a more specific version of Vygotsky's "instance-bound to principled shift". However, both stages of the "characteristic-to-defining feature" shift would seem to involve predication, for the notion of a "characteristic-to-defining feature" shift has built into it the assumption that words are in both instances applied on the basis of other predicates they are associated with; in the first stage, predicates for typical or characteristic features, and in the second, predicates for defining or essential features. The first stage of Vygotsky's "instance-bound to principled" shift, however, need not be supposed to involve predication since the distinction permits an interpretation like (2) above, a shift from names to predicates with semantic content; this interpretation of the "instance-bound to principled shift" as, roughly, the shift from phase 1 to phase 3, would reflect the proposed cognitive difference that superordination effects, from naming to predication. Thus, I think there is good reason to conclude that a "characteristic-to-defining feature" shift is not a version of Vygotsky's "instance-bound-to-principled" shift. So, on the current proposal, both stages of the former shift but not of the latter, belong properly to the post-superordinate stage, after genuine predication has been achieved. Thus, the evidence that Keil and Kelley review and that leads them to conclude that the shift is quite gradual and takes place at different times for different domains is not about the shift that superordination marks and does not conflict with Vygotsky's observations that a shift across all domains occurs roughly between ages five and seven.

25   Early Syntax

I return now to the question how we can reconcile the Superordination Hypothesis with the fact that pre-superordinate speech exhibits grammatical sentence structure. Although several qualifications must be made to the details of Vygotsky's analysis, he provides sound insight into the manner of this reconciliation; for his reflections suggest a conception of early syntax that coheres with the current proposal.

If we construe pre-superordinate speech as not genuinely exemplifying subject–predicate distinctions that occur in adult discourse, then we must also accept that some degree of mastery of linguistic structures is possible even though the words occurring in the child's structures do not actually function in the syntactic-semantic roles that they have in the language, in the linguistic community, and in adult discourse. Following Vygotsky, we may conclude that the child is able to use grammatical forms and structures correctly "before the child has understood the logical operations for which they stand. The child may operate with subordinate clauses, with words like because, if, when, and but, long before he really grasps causal, conditional, or temporal relations. He masters syntax of speech before syntax of thought" (Vygotsky, 1962, p. 46). Indeed, it seems hardly in need of empirical support that, in some sense, "the child begins to operate with concepts, to practice conceptual thinking, before he is clearly aware of the nature of these operations" (Vygotsky, 1962, p. 69).

We can agree that pre-superordinate speech displays some syntax where what is meant by this is that ordered patterns of words and particles are discernible; we may suppose even that these discernible patterns are communicatively meaningful for the child in a general non-linguistic sense. We might suppose, for example, that they are associated with the child's needs and wants including those to communicate needs and wants to others and the general human need to be in social communication with others, as long as we do not understand by this description anything that implies linguistic conceptualization by the pre-linguistic child.

Contrary to Vygotsky's claim, however, the evidence does not require us to suppose that there is anything that we should call "mastery of syntax" at the pre-superordinate stage, but only that there are patterns discernible in early speech, some but not all of which reflect the syntactic patterns of mature speech. That a child should be a competent imitator of patterns of action and movements that it perceives is a precondition of all human practical development so it is not surprising that imitation should be an important factor in the development of higher conceptual abilities and the linguistic skills that subtend them, in addition to its role in the development of less subtle and more obvious non-cognitive pattern-based abilities.[17] Of course, nothing said here precludes the possibility of innate syntax.

Another feature of Vygotsky's theory that cannot be accepted is his assumption that mature conceptualization is essentialist. The application of the Aristotelian-Thomistic concept of essences to the explanation of knowledge of word meaning has been favored throughout the development of empirical Realism. Desiring strong coherence with Realistic Logical Positivism, what I have called the Standard Theory (section 6) represents word meaning as normally consisting of a defining feature which might be understood as the natural essence of the items in the extension of a general term or as articulating the necessary and sufficient conditions for the correct use of the term (Carnap, 1928; Goodman, 1951; Katz and Fodor, 1964). Indeed, a conception of philosophical analysis robustly devolved upon this essentialist construal of linguistic conceptualization until very recently. This essentialist picture of what is known by an individual who knows a word's meaning has, however, been strongly discredited by recent studies in both psychology and philosophy (Rosch et al., 1976; Putnam, 1975; Wittgenstein, 1953).

From the perspective recommended here, Vygotsky's essentialist presupposition is a theoretical flaw that leads him to deny that the prerequisites to discursive thought are satisfied before late adolescence. If discursive (that is, linguistic) conceptualization is initiated with superordinate recognition and concomitant predication, essentialist conceptualization – interpreting predicates in accordance with unique defining characteristics – may nevertheless not become an entrenched practice until late adolescence. This too is not surprising since the idea that there *are* unique defining characteristics for some things is first explicitly met as a general practice (excluding such "single-criterion" words as kinship terms) in the study of the special sciences and this study is not generally begun until adolescence, long after superordination and fluency have been achieved. Essentialist conceptualization is distinct from superordination in several ways which suggest that it is reasonable to suppose that the latter is a precondition of the former. One difference is that superordination but not essentialist conceptualization presupposes a hierarchy with several orders (for example, the orders subordinate–basic–superordinate) and with elements, parts of which may be "in place" before they become reconfigured into a hierarchical structure as in, for example, *Wheaties, food, eat it*. Wheaties is no more essentially food than it is essentially groceries, manufactured, a brand of cereal, flakes, brown, edible, marketed, or breafast of champions, although each of these is superordinate to *Wheaties* and they occupy differing but overlapping orders; they are nodes within a network. Another difference between essentialist predication and superordination is that establishment of a particular superordinate hierarchy in an individual seems developmentally related to (that is, seems to depend upon there being) other such hierarchies with which it contrasts. With the achievement of superordination, a reorganization of conceptual elements – I should not say of concepts but only of elements, or of parts of elements, capable of being inserted into conceptual structures when other conditions are met – is effected. For example, the contrasts among *robin, bird, it flies* and *Wheaties, food, eat it* or *VW, car, drive it* may be supposed to reinforce (what we recognize as) the uniform pattern that they share. Essential properties are, by contrast, coextensive; anything of which *water* is truly predicated is something of which H_2O is truly predicated, we may say by way of illustration. Quite possibly co-extensionality (hence, essentialist conceptualization) is developmentally dependent upon superordinate achievement. It is easy to suppose that one cannot really entertain the notion that two predicates apply truly to exactly the same items until one has predication. For only if one has predication does one know words that apply truly to more than one subordinate type of item, each of which subordinate type applies to different individual items in virtue of the different superordinates that apply (truly) to the subordinate items. For example, *food* is superordinate to *Wheaties, meat, vegetables*; however, each of these is subordinate to *food* in virtue of other superordinates which they do not share. For these examples we have as contrasting superordinates (for example), respectively, *cereal, from an animal, from a garden*. Although *edible* is a superordinate for *food*, being edible is neither the essence of food nor an essential characteristic of food, for food can be administered through the veins in the form of a solution instead of being eaten, plants don't eat their food, candy, while edible, is not food, and so forth.[18]

The increased rate of growth in the mental lexicon that literacy makes possible may explain the noticeable increase in fluency that begins with formal education and there are no grounds for doubting that literacy facilitates the development of syntactic and logical skills. Nevertheless, the current proposal is that these are skills that are *initiated* via superordinate achievement independently of literacy.

26   But What Is Predication?

Just how interconnected our two questions (section 23) are may by now be altogether too clear to the reader who has perhaps been asking throughout this discussion of how we are to construe early speech, "But what is predication?" While it would be formally more satisfying immediately to offer an answer, the considerations just made require a more restrained approach to this question. Let me explain. It has throughout this essay been suggested that the logical and ontological categories in terms of which we describe ourselves and our pre-linguistic conspecifics make cavalier use of a form of projection that is difficult to describe directly. Russell's cavils against supposing that the grammatical form of our, mature, utterances reflect their logical structure present trivial difficulties compared with the problem presented by the disparity between the grammatical forms that we standardly attribute to the utterances that are produced by our pre-linguistic progeny and what all evidence reveals to be their impoverished cognitive acumen. I have argued that the key to understanding this disparity is the phenomenon of superordination, an achievement that is, for humans, tantamount to the achievement of predication. Nevertheless, it is not consistent with the hypotheses and data that I have described to assume that predication itself must be understood as a phenomenon that has a single and unique representation. So, as I turn now to address the pressing question "What is predication?", I ask the reader not to prepare for an answer that displays the standard features of essentialism: although there are preferred ways of representing both entry-level and higher cognitive functions, it is unwarranted to suppose that competing representations of these functions can be evaluated on a single dimension. For this reason, instead of asking directly what is the essence of predication, I propose to consider possible answers to the question "What is predication?" in the course of addressing the related developmental question, "What turns a response into an assertion?"

Notes

1   It does not, however, mark the onset of conscious life, nor, I should say, of thought. A distinction among sensory classes, perceptual categories, and conceptual categories will be introduced later in this essay that provides a basis for distinguishing between different forms of consciousness.

2   Macnamara's grouping here is puzzling. He says, "There is a strain of influential modern writing stemming, I believe, from Wittgenstein's *Philosophical Investigations* (1953) and strongly evident in the writings of Piaget . . . and Quine (especially 1973), that logical resources emerge from logic free activities. I find this writing hopelessly muddled" (1986, p. 29). But there is little relation apparent between Quine's view of the development of logical competencies and Wittgenstein's. The former supposes that a physicalist description of sensory input alone is sufficient for generating those capacities set-theoretically. Wittgenstein, however, completely diavows this possibility, focusing instead on the essential linguistic component of public social practices and on the limitations of then-current logical theory to describe perspicuously the changes wrought on the novice by these practices. It was, rather, his Tractarian view that was closest to Quine's.

3   I thank Peter Bretsky for calling this result to my attention.

4   I am not here endorsing Palmer's characterization, since it raises but does not address very complex problems about distinguishing meaning from truth, as well as general ontological questions about propositions.

5   I do not mean by these remarks to recommend a view that metaphors are equivalent in meaning to any literal statement, or indeed to recommend here any account of what metaphor is.

6   Note, however, that even contrasting views do accept some premises about language learning (ones I have claimed are false); for example, that it is to be explained fully by appealing to innate abilities.

7   On this fact, I agree with Macnamara (1986), but the argument sketched here does not accord with his proposal, for reasons I turn to in section 22.

8   This conclusion, inimical to the Standard Theory in all its forms of which I am aware, is suggested also by Vygotsky (1978, p. 45): "Although the indirect (or mediated [for Vygotsky, mediated by 'signs']) aspect of psychological operations is an essential feature of higher mental processes, it would be a great mistake, as I pointed out with respect to the beginnings of speech, to believe that indirect operations appear as the result of a pure logic. They are not invented or discovered by the child in the form of a sudden insight or lightening-quick guess (the so-called 'aha' reaction). The child does not suddenly and irrevocably deduce the relation between the sign and the method for using it. Nor does she intuitively develop an abstract attitude derived, so to speak, from 'the depths of the child's own mind.' This metaphysical view, according to which inherent psychological schemata exist prior to any experience, leads inevitably to an a priori conception of higher psychological functions."

9   Indeed, it is well known that at least some languages may not be best analyzed in terms of subject–predicate structures; see, for example, Li and Thompson (1978). I thank Leonard Rolfe for calling this issue to my attention, with regret that it cannot be pursued in greater detail here.

10   This suggestion is of course different from the claim made above that if one cannot entertain propositions then one cannot have any truth concept – or none that resembles in any important way a truth concept that we use. It seems obvious to me, if not to others, that very little that seems like discursive reasoning takes place before middle childhood – around age 7.

11   I am not here defending a skeptical position but only noting that the described dependency of entertaining propositions upon having a truth concept does not entail that anyone actually has knowledge of any truths.

12   The inadequacies of first-order logic in both formal semantics and in the theory of human language have been acknowledged by numerous theoreticians and to differing ends. Jon Barwise, for example, analyzes these as inadequacies of first-order logic (FOL) "and its extensions to other unsituated logics" in providing "a

fully adequate mathematical model of meaning" (Barwise, 1989, p. 295). While I shall have more to say about such formal matters later in this essay, the argument of the current section does not address these formal issues, even though it is relevant to them.

13   Indeed, the same can be noted concerning the question whether pre-linguistic humans and members of other species should be said to have beliefs. See, for example, Barcan Marcus (1990).

14   Our color *concepts*, incorporating a certain color taxonomy, have a degree of arbitrariness built into them, the difference between *red* and *orange* for example. This is part of the reason why 'red' is not, strictly speaking, the *name* of a sensum or qualia. It is a description of the color of some things.

15   The literature on mental content and on categorical perception are particularly noteworthy in this respect; in the case of the former, the explanation for this absence is almost certainly widespread adherence to the Standard Theory.

16   For the moment, I am using "predicate" and "general term" without reference to any particular analysis of them and with whatever ordinary sense they convey.

17   The topic of early childhood syntax is one that cannot be surveyed here. There is a large and growing literature on child syntax, with many different and conflicting theories advanced. Many of these have been constructed under the dominant paradigm of what I have called "The Standard Theory", but there is so much disagreement about this matter that I must avoid adding finer questions about child syntax to the present discussion than those relating directly to Vygotsky's general claims and the proposed hypothesis.

18   Another example of conceptual change resulting from technological advances: being a source of nutrition used to be an "essential" property of food but the pills and powders used today as sources of nutrition are *not* food.

5 From Response to Assertion

Awareness of truth and falsity is implicit in the assertoric use of language; "these two objects", Frege wrote, "are recognized, if only implicitly, by everyone who judges something to be true."
Michael Dummett, "Language and Truth"

Of the problems that are historically associated with efforts to understand human cognitive development from infancy, those arising from the necessity of using our mature conceptualizations to describe the contents of consciousness of the developing infant, *in re* so to speak, often seem insurmountable (section 21). And, as with many apparently insurmountable problems, the temptation for those post-behaviorists who are indeed convinced that the pre-linguistic infant together with members of non-language-using species nevertheless have active although limited conscious lives is to ignore these problems and to attribute to such conscious subjects whatever conceptual content we imagine that we ourselves would have were we, now, in their booties, located in their perspective, and behaving as they behave. No doubt there is also some efficiency in this strategy, just as there is in the fact that it is our second nature not to distinguish in consciousness at the time of discourse between the utterances we make and their meanings or referents. As this last oversight serves a utility of economy in brain use, so to assume homogeneity of mental life in infant and adult may serve utilities in the economy of social resources. We treat the child as having already achieved that which they must learn to become, thereby assisting their development in that direction. This strategy has the added benefit of a built-in prototype for interpersonal behavior for use in constructing our own conduct with them: treat them as you would treat those who think thus and so.[1]

But the central presupposition of this strategy does not survive even cursory reflection; the infant cannot have our conceptual content. Nevertheless, at some early stage in its development, the infant must have a mentality that is capable of sustaining development into the relatively rich conceptual product which we describe ourselves as embodying. On the course set by the Superordination Hypothesis, there is at least one crucial step in that developmental process, the internalization of predicative structures. It is time to address the question what predication is.

27 Is There a Transition from Response to Assertion?

The developmental analogue to the traditional philosophical question of what predication is, is the question what turns a verbal response into an assertion. The fact that this question presupposes a difference between a response and an assertion does not seem contentious, since many types of acts other than verbal ones clearly may constitute responses; for example, acts that comply with or dismiss a request. We do not suppose that all verbal acts of adults must be understood as assertions or as expressing judgments, so we should be prepared to allow that infant speech might be non-assertoric and more in the nature of responses.

We must consider, then, why the hypothesis that predication is a cognitive function that is acquired in the course of first-language learning should be at odds with a number of accounts of human understanding. The Standard Theory takes psychological structures that are isomorphic with propositional structures as given and so not in need of explanation. Thus, Miller and Johnson-Laird "include judgment in the process of perception itself":

> This . . . assumption would be that in order to make a discriminative response to stimulation, one has to attend to and make

judgments of various properties and relations offered by the perceived situation. For this reason we phrased our discussion of
sensation and perception in terms of perceptual predicates expressing judgments. ... The capacity to make a match/mismatch
judgment can be built into the theory at its foundations, obviating
the need to explain its development as a consequence of
learning.   (Miller and Johnson-Laird, 1976, pp. 692–3)

In this way the troublesome question "What turns a response
into an assertion?" is avoided altogether. In effect, this is the
question how a child can learn a (or the) truth predicate. How
does a child come to understand what truth is supposed to be?
To be sure, one need not employ the words 'true' and 'false' in
order to understand what truth and falsehood are, to have a
truth predicate. Such understanding can be manifested in many
ways other than explicit employment of these words and it is a
separate research project, largely an empirical one, to investigate
the ways in which such understanding is manifested. Common to
all of them, however, will be an ability to evaluate an utterance
on the dimension of its truth and falsehood as opposed to its
meaning, its acceptance, its reinforcement by others, or some
other personal utility.[2] But if this is roughly correct, then the
relevant ability presupposes an awareness of utterances as candidates for such evaluation.

The question "What turns a response into an assertion?" looms
large on associationist or reinforcement theories of learning language, for such theories describe early language learning as the
result of adult reinforcement of the relevant overt behavioral
responses to stimuli; the problem for such theories is then how
to account for the transformation of this reinforced behavior into
behavior in which the child is *asserting* that a proposition or
statement *is true*. If utterances are always mere reinforced responses to stimuli then not only are truth and knowledge chimerical but the utterance of claims that are not shared by one's
parental or peer community must be viewed always as obstinate
anti-social behavior, and never as a new light. That is to say,
beliefs also will be chimerical, even as phenomena or as artifacts
of Folk Psychology. But this is surely to go too far.

On the account given by Miller and Johnson-Laird, however,
"there is no evidence that the transition from response to

assertion that this theory is intended to explain ever occurs in the language learning of young children" (Miller and Johnson-Laird, 1976, p. 692). Accordingly, they build assertoric structure into their model of pre-linguistic perception. But the considerations of the last two chapters show that the hypothesis that predication is learned and that superordinate achievement is tantamount to learning predication does not conflict with their observation that the language learning of *very young* children does not exhibit a stage-like transition from response to assertion. If assertion is a cognitive achievement that is consequent upon superordination, then one must observe the young child (from two to five) *through middle childhood* (from five to eight) to find the evidence. The evidence is there, as we have seen in chapter 3, but it is subtle. In particular, the evidence is likely to be veiled by adherence to the Standard Theory.

In his later study, *Mental Models* (1983), Johnson-Laird has constructed a non-sentential account of the psychology of reasoning by interpreting the model-theoretic structures of Montague's possible-worlds semantics for (a part of) English as realistically representing mental structures. The non-sentential conceptual models introduced in this account do not themselves exhibit subject–predicate structure; rather, they are construed, set-theoretically, as completely denotational structures which satisfy the rigorous principle of compositionality that is found in set theory: as sets are identified and individuated in set theory solely by their component elements, so are the possible worlds and their contents in Montague's semantics and so also are the conceptual models and their contents in Johnson-Laird's application of Montague's semantics to psychological models of reasoning.[3] In defense of this structural property, Johnson-Laird says,

> Although there appears to be an important ontological difference between entities and their properties, and the two are certainly distinguished in perceptual models, there are no crucial differences in their logical behavior. I have therefore treated them uniformly in conceptual models. (If it were desirable to distinguish them, then it would be necessary to introduce machinery for conjoining properties to tokens representing individuals, for negating them, and so on.) (Johnson-Laird, 1983, p. 425)

One problem with this characterization is that of understanding what is meant by the assertion that "there are no crucial differences" in the logical behavior of entities and their properties. A model-theoretic semantics standardly presupposes set-theoretically represented propositions or propositional structures; so there will be assumed in the formal syntax for whose output the semantics provides an interpretation, rules for the well-formedness of formulae. Although these rules may be notationally different in different formulations of set theory, if they are rules for representing subject–predicate propositions, or, alternatively, entity–property relations, then they require informal understanding of such relationships. It is true that if we think of the actual world and of possible alternative worlds, we will likely think of collections of things dressed, so to speak, in their properties, perhaps with some of their properties "grafted" on to them.[4] Different possible worlds with the same things in them will have those things "wearing" different properties. So, within any world, things will be similar to some things and different from others by virtue of overlapping or discrete properties – where properties are themselves represented as sets that are completely defined by the entities that are their members in different possible worlds.[5] In this way, possible worlds semantics permits a quasi-extensional representation of different properties that resist differential representation in terms of real-world extensions. In our real world, some different properties are co-extensive; the extensions of 'animal with a heart' and 'animal with a kidney', and also 'unicorn' and 'centaur', are identical. Possible worlds are structures that can be fully described in terms of the sets of which individual things are or are not co-members. But it does not follow from the fact that we can represent properties as sets of things in different possible worlds that there is no logical difference between entities and their properties, for such a difference is presupposed by the whole endeavor. Indeed, it is the difference by means of which *different* possible worlds, some containing the same entities with different properties, can be constructed.

Johnson-Laird's reference to "entities and their properties" is *prima facie* a metaphysical (ontological) distinction, as opposed to the distinction between subjects and predicates which is, *prima facie*, a grammatical or syntactic distinction. There is no canonical interpretation of either pair of expressions and debates about relations between the two pairs have ebbed and flowed.

28   Subjects and Predicates

Efforts to say what predication is have largely been efforts to describe differences between subjects and predicates and these have been of two sorts, ontological and formal. Traditional philosophical problems devolving around the notions of subjects and predicates have most often been cast in an ontological form, the distinction between subjects and predicates being made in terms of the kinds of entities to which the expressions in those grammatical or logical roles were alleged to refer. It is particulars, referred to by singular terms and proper names, as opposed to their properties, referred to by general terms and common names, in terms of which the distinction has historically been cast. Thus, during his Logical Atomism period, Russell believed that in addition to particulars there must be universals to which the logical predicates of propositions, in contrast to what he considered the misleading grammatical predicates of sentences, refer. Frank Ramsey challenged such attempts to draw metaphysical conclusions from the syntax of propositions, arguing that every sentence was equivalent in meaning to another in which the predicate of the former is transformed into the subject of the latter. His remark was, "Now it seems to me as clear as anything can be in philosophy that the two sentences 'Socrates is wise', 'Wisdom is a characteristic of Socrates' assert the same fact and express the same proposition" (Ramsey, 1925, p. 21). Nevertheless, in more recent years, Strawson's study of the logic and grammar of subjects and predicates, while remarking on Ramsey's comment, also gives a characterization of the distinction that relies upon ontological differences, in this case between particulars and concepts: "Combine two expressions, one specifying the particular in question and one specifying the concept in question, in such a way that the result of the combination is true, or expresses a truth, if the particular exemplifies the concept – or, if the concept applies to the particular – and is false, or expresses a falsehood, if it does not" (Strawson, 1974, p. 21).

Quine has eschewed references to concepts and universals in the interest of avoiding ontological commitment to anything but terms or expressions and their extensions in the actual, physical world and has undertaken a number of characterizations of the difference between subjects and predicates intended to conform to this preferred "thin" ontology. One such characterization is this: "The basic combination in which general and singular terms find their contrasting roles is that of predication. . . . Predication joins a general term and a singular term to form a sentence that is true or false according as the general term is true or false of the object, if any, to which the singular term refers" (Quine, 1960, p. 90).

It is thus characteristic of attempts to distinguish between subjects and predicates within the confines of a referential semantics to make the distinction in terms of different ontological classes to which subject and predicate terms apply. Commonly, as in the cases at hand, the metaphysical assumptions that motivate the account are then concluded to be necessary preconditions of the phenomenon that is so accounted for (see, for example, Quine, 1974, and Strawson, 1959).

Neither Strawson's nor Quine's contextual characterizations of predicates and predication afford insight into the character of the infant's transition in its cognitive development to a propositional thinker, a thinker who has acquired the skill of predication. First, if either characterization were thought of as a production rule, then only one who already has a sentence recognition skill could use that rule in producing an assertion, for the user of such a rule must first judge that a sentence has been produced and only then can test the product to determine whether that sentence "is true or false according as the general term is true or false of the object, if any, to which the singular term refers." But, by hypothesis, the infant who does not have predication cannot recognize sentences. Second, each characterization makes essential use of the notions of truth and falsehood, but it has been argued (section 22) that these notions cannot be understood without some awareness of objects to be their bearers. Thus, although the notions of truth and falsehood might be understood, or even employed,

by one who has no specific word for them, one cannot understand them unless one also has some understanding of a class of
objects to which these apply. But the pre-superordinate infant has
no such understanding, *ex hypothesi*, and so cannot use truth or
falsehood in the manner prescribed by the purported rule to test
whether the general term is "true or false of the object, if any, to
which the singular term refers." Lastly, each characterization,
once again thought of as a production rule, requires its user to
understand what *referring* to objects or particulars consists in, an
understanding that seems unavailable to the infant.

In this assessment of Strawson's and Quine's descriptions of
predicates and predication for their possible use in answering the
question "What is predication?" in a way that might prove useful
in understanding both what the infant achieves and how it is
achieved, it is important to distinguish between the infant's
achieving a skill or ability and the infant's knowing the accepted
description of that skill or ability. In denying that the infant
could identify sentences and evaluate them as true or false prior
to having an ability to make predications, I am not making the
tautological remark that the infant could not use these *expressions*
correctly prior to understanding these expressions. Rather, I am
denying that the infant could identify or recognize members
of the class of assertoric sentences (or utterances) and evaluate
them as true or false without possessing the cognitive skill of
predication.

Of the cognitive skills mentioned in Quine's characterization,
one may come closer than the others to having an interpretation
in the range of the infant's abilities just prior to superordination;
this is recognition of an expression's being "true of" an object.
For it is clear that the child is, at this stage, aware of some
objects and aware also that some expressions are paired with
some objects while others are not paired with some objects. The
turn of phrase "true of" can certainly be used to describe the
relation of which the child is aware in these cases, but that relation bears little resemblance to the concept of truth according to
which sentences, utterances or propositions are true or false
simpliciter.[6] The relation of which the child is aware may be the
code relation whose inadequacy to sustain an acquisition theory
was probed in chapter 2.[7]

29   Formal Approaches to Predication

In Quine's work, singular terms are additionally contrasted with general terms in his description that a singular term "names or purports to name one and only one object" while a general term "is true of each, severally, of any number of objects" (Quine, 1960, p. 90). And later, after his Elimination of Singular Terms, Quine's characterization of the distinction is made in a formal rather than an ontological mode, in terms of expressions that can occur in formulae consisting of the existential quantifier, a bound variable and a single predicate. Predicates are here construed as "items of vocabulary which thus combine with quantifiers to yield a sentence" (Strawson, 1974, p. 13). This change in the form of Quine's distinction, from ontological to formal, marks a shift in his approach in the direction of what has come to be known as formal semantics of natural languages. Although formal semantics has a rich background in the history of logic, the aim of providing a completely formal theory of the relation between expressions of a natural language and their meanings (alternatively, of the features of expressions in a natural language in virtue of which they mean what they do mean) is a relatively new idea.[8] Unfortunately, formal approaches to predication fare, if anything, worse than ontological ones in revealing anything whatsoever about the possible character of the relevant transition in the child.

There are two major directions that have been followed in work on formal semantics of natural language: model-theoretic semantics as developed by Richard Montague and adapted more recently by Barwise and Perry as "situation semantics"; and truth-conditional semantics associated with the work of Davidson.[9]

A review of how predication is represented in each will reveal that these theories also do not contribute light to the present inquiry. Of course, the theories are not to be faulted for this fact, and cannot be judged deficient for failing to do what they were never intended to do. Indeed, it is difficult to provide any rationale that would link up the problems of language acquisition theory with formal semantics. Nevertheless, formal semantics must be considered here, not only because we are searching high and low for some account of predication that might be relevant to understanding the developmental step that has been hypothesized, but also because theoreticians of cognitive development, empirical and philosophical, have themselves been influenced by these formalisms.

Davidson's truth-conditional semantics focuses centrally on the logical forms of sentences and aims to account for all that might be accounted for by a theory of meaning in terms only of logical form and conditions under which sentences are true – truth conditions – thus dispensing, like Quine, with meaning as an ontological category. Essentially, 'predicate' is a primitive category of expression within the formalism, to be given an analysis only informally, perhaps along the lines begun by Quine described above. Many linguists have made use of Davidson's conception of formal semantics, in part for the reason that it coheres so well with the conception of the logical form of sentences as the level of linguistic analysis that Chomsky had labelled "deep structure" in his standard grammar (Chomsky, 1965).

Model-theoretic semantics comes in different versions, of which the most famous is Montague's. His is, fundamentally, a possible-worlds semantics, aiming to interpret the meanings of sentences in a natural language in terms of sets of individuals in different possible worlds. A one-place predicate is a function from individuals to truth values, for each possible world (Dowty, et al., 1981, p. 83). The intension (meaning) of a predicate is a property. "Thus the property corresponding to the English *is asleep* can be thought of as the function which gives, for each possible situation, the set of individuals that are asleep in that situation" (Dowty, et al., 1981, p. 147). Here, a situation is interpreted as a possible world.

In contrast to Montague semantics, Barwise and Perry's situation semantics is a model-theoretic semantics that aims to make do without possible worlds and to substitute for them the notion of situations, preferably ones in the actual world. "The primitives of our theory are all real things: individuals, properties, relations, and space-time locations. Out of these and objects available from the set theory we construct a universe of abstract objects, situation types, *coe*'s [courses of events], event-types, and so on. Our aim is to have every component of the semantic theory be one of these abstract objects" (Barwise and Perry, 1983, p. 178). Thus, what Barwise and Perry called the "ecological realism" of situation semantics lies in the fact that it is not in the first instance about expressions in a language, as is Montague's version of model-theoretic semantics, but about "real things". So, strictly speaking, the theory says nothing about predicates but only about properties. Properties "like the property of being asleep" are identified with one-place relations in the system (Barwise, 1989, p. 50). Barwise neatly characterizes the feature in virtue of which model-theoretic semantics differs from truth-conditional semantics: "Within the model-theoretic tradition, valid entailments are valid not in virtue of form, but in virtue of content" (Barwise, 1989, p. 4), where the content is interpreted mathematically (rather than logically) in terms of sets of individuals, "with truth an important but derivative notion" (Barwise, 1989, p. 8).

Unfortunately, nothing here helps to answer the question "What is predication?" within the present context. This excursion into contemporary formal semantics is, however, not wasted but may help in understanding the two directions in which developmental theories have moved (perhaps more as well).[10] Nevertheless, neither direction within formal semantics seems capable of accommodating any representation of a cognitive shift from response to assertion or of throwing light on an alternative explanatory course.

30   Sensation, Perception, Conception, and Judgment

Normally we distinguish between sensation and perception in complex and multi-functional organisms according as the response that is evidence for either is a local response by some part of the organism or a general response of the whole organism. Such reflex responses as withdrawing the hand from a hot object are clear examples of the former while fleeing from a predator is normally an example of the latter. A response that is a general response of a whole complex organism (evidence of perception) requires for its explanation some reference to central processing by the organism because a complex organism is presumed to require some way of coordinating its various parts in order to make a whole-organism response.

The Standard Theory conflates perception and conception by supposing that whenever there is a general, whole-organism response, a *judgment* about the character of the stimulus must intervene between stimulus and response, a generalization that will send appropriate information to each part of the organism involved in the response.[11] In this way, judgment – as generalization – is built into pattern recognition and perception by the Standard Theory. Predication, if it is construed at all, is construed as categorization and categorization is taken to be a single central function of an organism whereby distinguishable stimuli are understood and responded to as if they were identical.[12] Miller and Johnson-Laird discount any developmental distinction between response and assertion because many responses are categorial in that they can only be understood as whole-organism responses to some generalized perception involving pattern recognition by the organism as a whole and thus as involving central processing.

These issues require a reconsideration of the phenomena of categorization. Instead of lumping together all evidence of categorization – from pattern recognition through early speech to categorial judgment – and supposing that a single account can or must be provided for all of them, different sorts of categorization can be more finely distinguished than they are on this account. On the progression from sensation to judgment, the crucial cut for distinguishing mere responses from assertions in the human natural world is the cut between perceptual categories and conceptual categories. Can a principled theoretical distinction, even a tentative one, be made between these two types of categories?

31 Categories of Perception, Categories of Conception

Any effort to describe such a difference between perceptual categories and conceptual categories is confronted with the following dilemma: In humans, the *best* evidence for categorization is linguistic evidence – what category the subject says an object belongs to. But in non-language-using species, the *only* evidence that categorization has occurred is the occurrence of a non-linguistic whole-organism response. So, either one makes the *ad hoc* decision to count only linguistic evidence as acceptable evidence of conceptual categorization or one treats perceptual and conceptual categories as substantially equivalent. To take the first course seems to prejudice the investigation in favor of humans, supposing perhaps gratuitously that only humans could enjoy the privilege of conceptualization, while taking the second course seems to prejudice the investigation against humans, supposing perhaps gratuitously that language is, after all, merely an efficient technology for communicating information that is intrinsically language-independent.[13]

Despite this problem, however, a distinction between perceptual and conceptual categories would provide a basis for a "thicker" account of superordinate (and subordinate) acquisition, one that might sustain an answer to the pressing question: "What is predication?" The language initiate, recall, is confronted with the fact that 'A robin is a bird' is accepted as an utterance but 'A bird is a robin' is not accepted. The latter is, let us suppose, negatively reinforced while the former is positively reinforced. Were the mechanisms at work in this situation merely mechanisms of response reinforcement, however, it would be difficult to see how the initiate would ever get the right idea – that *bird* is superordinate to *robin* – rather than, say, that to utter 'A bird is a robin' constitutes behavior that will be punished if one is caught saying it! To "get the right idea", the child must refrain not merely from uttering 'A bird is a robin' within parental earshot, the child must not do anything that could count as *entertaining the thought* that a bird is a robin. Not even in private.

To consider this situation from a slightly different perspective, what is at issue is not merely the unacceptability of an overt response. Acceptability and unacceptability of overt behaviors admit of degrees and are relative to contexts; what is highly unacceptable at the dinner table may be appropriate and expected behavior at a picnic. The contrast between what the child must eventually achieve in the way of cognitive development and a mere reinforced response, even a whole-organism response, is ultimately characterized by the adult language community in terms of bivalent truth: it is not true that a bird is a robin; and also that this is not because 'bird' and 'robin' are names of different items – for it is true that a robin is a bird and not true that birds are non-robins – but because *bird* is superordinate to *robin*.

32 The Generality Constraint

A principle introduced by Gareth Evans which he called "The Generality Constraint" suggests a direction in which we might find a satisfactory distinction between perceptual and conceptual categories (Evans, 1982). Although he introduced this principle in a context different from this one – in the course of discussing Russell's theory of singular terms – and with quite different theoretical goals from those that I am concerned with here, Evans was also keenly aware of the importance of distinguishing between perception and conception. Indeed, G. R. Gillett argues for the stronger conclusion that there is a conceptual relation between this constraint and the idea of a conscious thinking subject (Gillett, 1987). Here, then, is the Generality Constraint:

> . . . if a subject can be credited with the thought that *a* is *F*, then he must have the conceptual resources for entertaining the thought that *a* is *G*, for every property of being *G* of which he has a conception. This is the condition that I call 'The Generality Constraint'. (Evans, 1982, p. 104)[14]

According to this constraint, what distinguishes true conceptual thinkers from "mere responders or information processors" (Gillett, 1987, p. 20) is that predicates available to the thinker must stand in contrastive relations *for the thinker* to other predicates available to the thinker:

> Even readers not persuaded that any system of thought must conform to the Generality Constraint may be prepared to admit that the system of thought we possess – the system that underlies

the use of language – does conform to it. (It is one of the fundamental differences between human thought and the information-
processing that takes place in our brains that the Generality
Constraint applies to the former but not to the latter. . . .)   (Evans,
1982, p. 104, n. 22)

The suggestion that Evans's Constraint provides is that, while
both perceptual and conceptual categories are abstractions, only
conceptual categories must satisfy the Generality Constraint. For
a subject to have a concept, hence to use a general term in a
predicative judgment, the subject must satisfy the Generality
Constraint with respect to that concept or term.

33   Developmental Data

Recent work in developmental psycholinguistics suggests how
conceptual categories may be layered on top of and also interact
with perceptual categories in the first-language learner.

The level of categorization that Rosch et al. (1976) described
as basic and primary constitutes a level of abstraction, for us, of
general terms that is characteristically the first level in the
superordinate–subordinate hierarchy of a language whose terms
are used by the first-language learner. It is also the level of terms
selected by members of the language community at large when
they are queried in a non-directive way to say what some object
is, and of course, it is the level of terms used most often by
parents in talking to young children. Thus 'dog' and not its
superordinate 'animal' or its subordinate 'Collie' is the most likely
response when one is presented with a picture of a Collie and
asked, baldly, to say what kind of thing is depicted.

Efforts to determine distinctive features of this basic level of
categorization have yielded, according to Rosch, four converging
characterizations. The basic level is the most inclusive level of
categorization at which objects have numbers of *attributes in
common*; it is the most general level of classification at which
objects have associated *motor sequences in common*; it is a level
of greatest *increase of similarity in shape* (for example, there is
a greater increase of visual shape similarity from *animal* to *dog*

than there is from *dog* to *Collie*); the basic level is the most inclusive level at which the averaged *shape of an object can be
recognized* (Rosch, 1978).

These empirical data encourage the hypothesis that such basic
conceptual categories as *dog, cat, car, bus, chair, sofa* are ones
that are, with certain additional constraints, most highly congruent with perceptual categories which allow a high degree of mastery
independently of their correlative conceptual categories. "Mastery" here refers only to the ability to apply the terms to objects
that are in their extensions while refraining from applying them
to items that are not in their extensions.

Many other studies also enhance the conclusion that in early
language what are for adults general terms for conceptual categories are used as labels for some sensory presenta that are
perceived as the same.

Clark (1987) has shown that young children reject any apparent synonyms. If they already have one word for an object, their
strategy is to presume that a new word to be learned is not a
label for that object. They narrow down overextensions as they
acquire new, contrasting vocabulary items. Clark introduces a
"Principle of Contrast" to explain the child's early learning of
linguistic semantic categories: Difference in the form of language
entails difference in meaning. This statement of the Principle of
Contrast is, in the present context, imprecise, for the sense of
"meaning" that is implied is reference rather than linguistic semantic meaning (that is, "word meaning" or conceptual content).

Markman and Wachtel (1988) confirm that children initially
reject a second label for an object. They postulate an assumption
of taxonomic organization which they call the "Principle of Mutual Exclusivity": Assume category terms are mutually exclusive.
This, they argue, is a safe strategy for the language learner to
adopt since many categories, especially basic level ones (cf. Rosch
et al., 1976) and natural kinds (for example, cows, birds and
dogs) are mutually exclusive.

These studies were neither motivated by nor, of course, applied
to the current hypothesis, namely, that very early word usage,
in contexts of immediate perception, serve the formation of
perceptual categories as distinct from and as precondition to the
subsequent formation of conceptual categories.[15]

34 From Perceptual Categories to Conceptual Categories

The strategies that these principles account for do not by themselves yield successful and full entry into the language (cf. Anglin, 1977, and Keil, 1979). As noted earlier (chapter 3), overextensions and underextensions prevail; speech exhibits instance-orientation to concrete objects; and when rudimentary sentence structure is manifested, subjects and predicates are initially treated as symmetrical (cf. Strawson, 1971). It is only with the achievement of some hierarchies of superordinate terms that the conditions for satisfying the Generality Constraint appear: asymmetries of subjects and predicates together with contrastive sets of category terms and a degree of stimulus freedom not previously manifested. Let us now consider again the question: How does this hierarchical development occur?

We may suppose that the language novice is channeled, in the normal arrangement of its environment by members of the language community, to attend selectively to certain recurrent presented patterns. These recurrent patterns are associated with recurrent auditory patterns – words and simple combinations of words – the reproduction of which by the infant is reinforced, not necessarily explicitly. This complex of auditory, motor, and other arrangements results in early labelling, further entrenching for the infant the perceptual categories of the community that are engaged in the complex of arrangements. Thus do basic terms emerge first as labels for perceptual categories.

It is not until this store of perceptual categories becomes embedded, for the child, within the superordinate and subordinate categories of the target language that general terms, as predicates, emerge in the individual, and conceptual categories that satisfy the Generality Constraint appear. This process requires the language initiate to integrate its perceptual categories into the distributive and contrastive sets of conceptual categories of the full-fledged hierarchical structure. Indeed, it is the preexistence of these distributive and contrastive sets that undermines the infant's earlier strategy of attempting to match words and concatenations of words with its perceptual categories. Overextension and underextension prevail until the recognition that the utterances of some words (by others in the linguistic community) may be what distinguishes members of perceptual categories that are otherwise undistinguishable to the child. Thus, as noted earlier, Wheaties is food, because edible, and groceries, because purchased, and cereal, because a grain product.

35 The Emergence of Predication

Predication is thus a cognitive function that emerges in the course of first language learning. It consists in the assignment of linguistic semantic content – the ontogenesis of intensional meaning – to proto-predicates. Morphemes previously assigned only perceptual content acquire conceptual content by being associated in a particular way with other morphemes previously also assigned only perceptual content. Both perceptual prototypes and coding functions are relevant in understanding this progression, since the child must first associate its proto-predicates with discriminated stimuli or clusters of stimuli in order for this development to take place, and then the child must associate its proto-predicates with other ("second-order") proto-predicates, that is, superordinates. For purposes of this preliminary sketch, differences of logical structure among proper names, definite and indefinite descriptions are not represented. If the proposals made in this essay are roughly correct, something *like* unique reference is, psychologically, the default value of pre-superordinate speech.

We may thus hypothesize three stages to this development, with definite transitions between each stage:

Stage 1: Discriminating stimulus clusters;
Stage 2: Referring to intentional objects;
Stage 3: Predication.

Here is a fuller description, to a simple first approximation, of these stages and the transitions between them:

Stage 1: *Discriminating stimulus clusters*: focusing attention; developing perceptual constancy.

This is a stage prerequisite to the development of perceptual categories. Items in the environment are highlighted for the infant's attention by motor and auditory arrangement of the environment. Normally, sound sequences are used to direct the infant's attentional patterns.

Transitional phase: Linguistic stimuli as attentional intensifiers; developing prototypes in constructing intentional objects (object constancy).

Stage 2: *Referring to intentional objects*: prototypes as perceptual categories.

Perceptual categories that are coincident with the community's conceptual categories are reinforced, verbally and otherwise; early utterances of single words and patterned strings are efforts to code-pair perceived sound categories with other perceptual categories. While these efforts are initially successful for communicating a limited range of messages, they ultimately fail, resulting in over- and under-projections of the conceptual categories of the community.

Transitional phase: Distinguishing sentence negation from predicate negation (*Not: A bird is a robin ≠ A bird is a non-robin*); emergence of hierarchical structures of superordinate and subordinate categories; class inclusion; distributional sets.

Stage 3: *Predication*: Emergence of semantic entailments (for example, *If a VW is a car then a VW is a vehicle*); truth and falsehood; assertion and other preconditions for logical relations.

For humans, on this schematism, the cut between perceptual categories and conceptual categories is mediated by stage 2. These stages, however, do not have clear counterparts among non-humans for each stage is dependent for its normal development upon linguistic input from the social community. At stage 1 this linguistic input is needed to ensure satisfaction of the perceptual preconditions to language entry, in particular, a rich store of perceptual categories shared with the linguistic community.

Items to which the infant's attention is (advertently or inadvertently) directed are not necessarily named items – animal sounds, vehicle sounds, and noises associated with expressions of emotion may direct the infant's attention to some perceptual stimulus for its development of perceptual categories. At stage 2, the categories shift from being largely perceptual categories associated by the community with a sound pattern (linguistic or other) to being perceptual categories for prototypes of *conceptual* categories of the linguistic community – those conceptual categories represented in the community's lexicon that are closest to isomorphism with perceptual categories that the infant has already developed. On this model, prior to stage 3, verbal behavior by the language learner must be understood as response only rather than as assertion of (the truth or falsehood of) a statement, no matter how syntactically complex it may be. Conceptual categories emerge only with stage 3, when the numerous purely perceptual categories are reconfigured into the necessary hierarchy for predication, as a forced option apparently, for solving the problem of unacceptable utterances.

It would be a mistake to suppose that the earlier stages drop out of the language learner's repertoire once stage 3 is entered, for the evidence is that both stage 1 and stage 2 activities may continue throughout life. This suggestion actually amounts to no more than the suggestion that our human cognitive life is not exclusively propositional. The propositional part remains as overlay upon the strategies embodied in the earlier stages.

While this schematic requires considerable refinement, perhaps correction, its general outline promises to yield accounts of numerous details about our cognitive and discursive practices that have been obscure, at best, or else downright mysterious on the Standard Theory.

36 Some Consequences of "Thick" Superordination

The considerations made so far, in particular, the relevance of the Generality Constraint, suggest resolutions to several problems;

two of these will now be mentioned in concluding this chapter, with others to be described in the following chapter.

First, there is the problem of the contrasts between linguistic communication and animal communication described in chapter 1 (section 2). What was there described as the determinateness of animal communication in contrast with the indeterminateness of the comparable linguistic communication is a function of the satisfaction of the Generality Constraint by the latter but not by the former. The linguistic communication is not related to a determinate response in the way that an animal's cry or signal is related to a determinate response for the following reason. The fact that one property is truly predicable of something leaves open the possibility that any particular response to that property may be counterindicated by some *other* property that may also be truly predicated of that thing. What is an antelope may be too high in cholesterol, already claimed by a more powerful predator, and so on. This consequence of our interpretation of the Generality Constraint suggests two related principles. First, there is the Generality of Predicables Principle:[16]

Any subject that has a property has more than one property.

Second, there is another principle in play to the effect that knowledge that a subject has one property is not, in general, sufficient to determine a specific response to that subject. We need, that is, a principle to account for the decouplings of stimuli from responses in the case of linguistic communication and, more generally, propositionally represented information. As a start, we may frame a Principle of Response Generality:

The fact that a subject has a certain property does not alone entail any specific response to that subject.

Alternatively, we might call such a principle "The Principle of Response Unboundedness of Predication".

A second feature discussed in the foregoing that is related to the Generality Constraint is the uncodeliness of linguistic communication in this respect: there is no one-to-one correlation between the semantic elements of a language and items in the world that are uniformly identifiable by random members of a language community independently of and prior to the acquisition of a language (chapter 2; chapter 3, section 12). It is not necessary to invoke another principle to relate the Generality Constraint to this fact. We can, instead, explain this fact directly by the Generality Constraint if we make appropriate and motivated modifications to it.

Evans described his constraint as applying to the system of thought we possess and this system of thought, in turn, as "the system that underlies the use of language". I am arguing that this very system of thought, instead of being a precondition for the use of language, is itself a partial product of the system of language practices in which we acquire the means to take part. I say "partial" product because it is of course true that we are organisms capable of attaining this product in contrast with members of other species, so there are certainly preconditions on organism types, and likely predispositions, involved in this attainment. Accordingly, I want to incorporate the Generality Constraint into the description of what is achieved in the transition from response to assertion. This construal does not preclude its use also as a defining condition of "conceptual thought". Nevertheless, my appropriation of Evans's constraint requires some modifications, one of a sort which can easily be made if his form of description is retained, but others of a sort that would require the introduction of extensive technical apparatus and devices that would not substantially augment, and would almost certainly obscure, the positive argument underway. Accordingly, I shall retain the form of description that Evans has used, with the general qualification that this description is intended now to describe the *results of acquiring* conceptual structures that are implicit in the discourse practices of a linguistic community.

One of the modifications required is that the constraint must be relativized to appropriate domains of subject–property pairs as well as to an appropriate variety of such pairs. If one is to be credited with *asserting* that, for example, a robin is a bird, then one must have the conceptual resources for entertaining such thoughts as the thought that a robin is, for example, an animal, but surely not for entertaining the thought that a robin is a VW! However, one must also have the conceptual resources for entertaining analogously structured thoughts such as that Wheaties is cereal and that a VW is a car. The general idea is suggested by the following:

> If a subject can be credited with asserting that x is F then she must have the conceptual resources for entertaining the thought that x is G, for every property of being G of which she has a conception and which is within the semantic domain of 'x'; and for entertaining, for some y that is not within the semantic domain of 'x', that y is H.

The expressions for which 'x', 'F', 'G', 'y', and 'H' are place-indicators in this schema will be themselves artifacts of the relevant language, independently of the naturalistic or non-naturalistic status of their referents and meanings in what we may call, following Chomsky, the E-language (that is, the external, public language of the mature speakers of a language). A coding theory of language learning must suppose innate knowledge of such artifacts, and this is an impossible supposition.

Notes

1   Numerous accounts of those who abuse their children display alarming results of supposing that children who do something that annoys their caretaker conceptualize their situation and their behavior in the way that an adult so placed and so acting may be expected to conceptualize them. The Victorian conception of children as having the minds of adults but errant wills is another startling example of this tendency. One wants to ask, "How could they *believe* this in the face of the counter evidence?"

2   Once again, it should be noted that nothing said here implies that we know any truths or that the child capable of assertion has discovered some truths.

3   See Montague's characterization of his semantics quoted in chapter 3.

4   Their "essential" properties.

5   For simplicity in exposition, I leave out of consideration at this point the problems associated with the fact that possible worlds semantics fails to make certain desirable distinctions among properties – for example, if there are no unicorns and no centaurs in any possible world, then the property of being a unicorn and that

of being a centaur will be represented as identical properties, as will be all "impossible" properties, having the same, null, membership, even though they are conceptually distinct.

6 The view just stated is different from a position explored in my "Truth and Sentences" (1969), where I try to derive *is true* from *is true of*. The main argument of that paper is that sentence utterances can be construed as bearers of truth and falsehood, a view I defend also in *Foundations for an Adequate Criterion of Paraphrase* (1970) and with which I am still in agreement.

7 In "Truth and Sentences" (1969), I argued against the need to posit propositions as bearers of truth and falsehood, in the spirit of a sparser ontology. What I now think those considerations show is that in order to understand propositions to be the bearers of truth and falsehood, humans must first take these to be features of utterances of sentences.

8 This is not the place to review the history of formal semantics, but some historical landmarks can be cited. These must include Carnap's *Meaning and Necessity* (1947), Tarski's "The Semantic Conception of Truth" (1944) and his "The Concept of Truth in Formalized Languages" (1956) and Kripke's provision of a formal semantics for modal logic, informally introduced as a semantics in terms of possible worlds, in "Semantical Considerations on Modal Logic" (1963) following his "A Completeness Theorem in Modal Logic" (1959).

9 There are also more recent variations on these now classic approaches but it would take us too far afield of our current concern to venture into them, but see Bealer (1982) and Bealer and Mönnich (1989) for one important new direction.

10 An interesting attempt to display formal differences among three theories of predication has been made by Nino Cocchiarella in *Logical Investigations of Predication Theory and the Problem of Universals* (1986). I have decided not to include discussion of Cocchiarella's work here out of concern that it would sidetrack us into issues that cannot be given their due within current constraints. I briefly note, however, that he is not so much concerned with what the cognitive skill of predication is as he is with describing three different ontologies subscribed to by different philosophers in their treatment of predication. The position of this essay is perhaps closest to what he calls "Conceptualism" as opposed to "Realism" and "Nominalism", but this is a simplification.

11 Dretske presents this charge against "information-processing models of mental activity", that is, that they "tend to conflate perceptual

and sensory phenomena on the one hand with cognitive and conceptual phenomena on the other" (1981, p. 135). His solution is to distinguish, in his own information-processing model, between analog (perceptual) and digital (conceptual) codings of information, a fair enough solution, but one that does not confront the naturalistic problems of supposing that a language is a code that were discussed in chapter 2.

12 The question by whom the stimuli are distinguishable, observed organism or observing researcher, is best allowed, here, to remain in its murky state.

13 This dilemma is apparent in many of the entries in Stevan Harnad's excellent and innovative collection, *Categorical Perception* (1987c).

14 Note that Evans's constraint is proposed for singular propositions, as is indicated by his use of the individual constant 'a' in subject position. For present purposes, it would be more natural to use the variable 'x' in subject position. Evans was principally interested in stating a condition for a thinker to be able to have a thought about a particular individual.

15 The research results of Hart and Gordon (1992) that were described in the preceding chapter suggest further possibilities for empirically testing the hypothesis that perceptual categorization in humans is a cognitive function that is distinguishable from conceptual, language-mediated, categorization. Newton Garver has remarked that the differences between defining the positive integers in terms of congruent sets, Russellian-style, and defining them by axioms, as Peano did, may parallel such a distinction – the former being visually based and the latter language-based.

16 It is tempting to call this principle "The Anti-Plato" and the subsequent principle "The Anti-Skinner".

6 Discursive Practices

Different persons growing up in the same language are like different bushes trimmed and trained to take the shape of identical elephants. The anatomical details of twigs and branches will fulfill the elephantine form differently from bush to bush, but the overall outward results are alike.

W. V. Quine, Word and Object

The foregoing proposals concern the relevance of language learning to the creation of cognitive structures in the individual, structures that subtend our human forms of life. It is evident from the support of these proposals proffered by results from developmental research that they have empirical ramifications. Nevertheless, they are put forth here as philosophical claims. What I mean by this qualification is that their form is too general – also, no doubt, too vague – for them to yield one way or the other to direct empirical test; and that their relations to other issues currently subject to dispute is broad-ranging. As for their feature of generality, it is hoped that they are less general than other proposals of a similar nature and that this fact may give rise sooner rather than later to experimental design aimed at testing one or another more precise description of these alleged phenomena. For example, if the Superordination Hypothesis is roughly correct, then it may be expected that some infants do not manage to make this transition in language development and this possibility as well as its causes may be amenable to testing, perhaps even to correction. As for the broader ramifications of these proposals, some reflections on them will now be offered to the patient reader who has trudged thus far in spite of the absence of formalisms and the abundance of generalizations. An additional caveat is required. The reflections to follow are made tentatively and as mere glimpses beyond the specific developmental issue of how we may understand language acquisition that has occupied the last three chapters. As such, they are suggested directions for future research and inquiry rather than conclusions yielded by the foregoing. What they have in common is that each reveals an intersection of our discursive practices with our knowledge practices. To speak in Quine's topiary metaphor, each reveals a curve taken by the twigs and branches that brings it closer to its "elephantine form".

37   Mutant Predicates

One major philosophical problematic in modelling the rational structures supposed implicit in discursive understanding has been the question of what distinguishes the peculiar predicates introduced by Goodman (1955) from the predicates that we accept as normal in our cognitive confrontations with phenomena that we wish to understand, theorize, and draw conclusions about. We seem to be in the same epistemic relation to the mutant property of being "grue" – where this predicate is defined as applying to all things examined before a certain time t just in case they are green but to other things just in case they are blue – as we do to such a normal property as being blue. Yet our rational practices reject grue-like properties. They have been dubbed "non-lawlike" and "unprojectible", but the question what exactly it is about their structure or content that distinguishes them from normal predicates has remained problematic. The hypotheses proposed here have a bearing on this issue. In particular, they suggest that a language whose normal predicates were grue-like could not be learned by humans as we are now constituted. If a first-language learner were normally confronted with utterances whose predicates were grue-like, then the problem described in the preceding chapters, which it is proposed that the child solves by acquiring superordination, either could not arise or could not be so solved.

There are numerous features of grue-like predicates that disqualify them as candidate general terms for initial acquisition of superordination. One is that their correct use is dependent upon knowledge of times and on understanding exclusive alternation, the 'either–or but not both' relation. It is apparent that the pre-superordinate language learner has no understanding of either feature which it might draw upon in order to learn the correct use of grue-like predicates. If the predicates commonly encountered by the first-language learner were standardly grue-like then the learner could not acquire superordination. Language entry, as marked by predication, would be precluded merely by the disjunctive character of such predicates. But there are more subtle features of such predicates which disqualify them, features which the present study places in sharper relief.

The respects in which grue-like predicates are in fact abnormal can be seen by considering their structural relations to other general terms. 'Grue' is not a "transcendental" term that names a highest genus; it does not hypothetically apply to everything and cannot, for this reason, be expected to have no superordinates. Hence, it should have or admit superordinates to which it is subordinate. What then is a candidate superordinate for *grue*? 'Grue' is not a color term: although things may change in color, colors do not change in color.[1] So *color* cannot be a superordinate for *grue*. To answer this question, then, to find a superordinate for *grue*, we must resort to other "mutant" predicates, such as 'timecolor'. But the language initiate could not learn the asymmetric hierarchical relations between *grue* and *timecolor* prior to some mastery of time relations. Indeed, the beginner who was following the strategy hypothesized in chapter 3 could, in fact, be learning only the predicate 'green' in any of its successful labeling efforts prior to the occurrence of the indexed time for the predicate 'grue', even though it would call green "grue".

Likewise, normal predicates that do not name highest genera have companion subordinates, other predicates that are encompassed by the same superordinate(s); in fact, it is essential to the ultimate success of the outlined strategy that there should be companion subordinates that exclude one another. This requirement is a developmental analog of the fact that the number of possible alternative words that fit a sentential context can be taken to be a measure of a word's information content in a context (Dretske, 1981) as well as being relevant to determining a word's semantic content (Ziff, 1960).[2] The notion of an *exclusionary companion subordinate* can be understood as a pragmatic partial interpretation of the formal semantic notion of a contrastive set. So, *robin* and *bluejay* are exclusionary companion subordinates of the superordinate *bird*; *horse* and *dog* are exclusionary companion subordinates of the superordinate *animal* (as well as, of course, *mammal*, *organism* and so forth). To find exclusionary companion subordinates for *grue*, however, it is obvious that we must once again turn to other mutant predicates under the mutant superordinate predicate 'timecolor', for example, the mutant predicates 'bleen' (examined before the indexed time and found to be blue, or else green) and 'rellow'. Each of these would, however, present the same practical impossibility for initial language entry as would 'grue'.

Finally, in order for humans to enter the hierarchical network structure of general terms by acquiring superordination in the manner proposed, not only must general terms have exclusionary companion predicates at the same level of the hierarchy, as 'grue' might have the mutant companions 'bleen' and 'rellow', but also general terms must be capable of being truly predicated of something. In order that the hypothesized problematic should present itself (non-propositionally) to the language learner there must be candidate subject terms some of which can be combined grammatically with the predicate terms to yield true statements. So, *food* is subordinate to *edible*, *Wheaties* is subordinate to *food* and *Wheaties is food* is true. Recall that the problem situation for the initial language learner is to learn that *Food is Wheaties* is, by virtue of the hierarchical relations between *food* and *Wheaties*, not true: *Wheaties* is not a superordinate of *food*, so 'Wheaties' cannot be predicated truly of food. But of what can 'grue' be truly predicated? If the indexed time for *grue* is prior to now, the first second of the year 1993, say, then *Emeralds are grue* is known to be false since emeralds examined for color since the first second of 1993 have been found not to be blue. In fact, no normal (non-grue-like) general term is a candidate for subject position in a true sentence with a grue-like predicate if the indexed time of the predicate is the first second of 1993, or any time sufficiently earlier to the present time, and items in the extension of the general term have been subsequently examined and found not to have the relevant mutant property. Once again we must resort to mutants such as 'emersapphires', now to find a candidate subject term for grue-predication. However, our attention has been shifted to the indexed time for *emersapphires*. Of course, if emersapphires are exactly those gemstones that are examined before the indexed time and found to be green emeralds or else are blue sapphires, the relevant indexed time would be the same as for *grue*, if it were true that emersapphires are grue. But it is obvious that 'emersapphires' inherits all the problems for the first-language learner of the other mutant general terms. A language whose normal general terms were like these mutants in the described respects could not be learned by humans like us (although it might be learned by bizarro-humans).

It will be noticed that this analysis of what is faulty with grue-like predicates does not engage such metaphysical or epistemic issues as whether it is true that the future will be like the past or whether our inductive hypotheses are justified, the original stage settings for 'grue'. Questions about the conditions required for language entry as construed here are instead pragmatic ones about the preconditions for such metaphysical and epistemic discourse, for they are about the preconditions of human discourse. Equally, they are pragmatic questions in another sense of "pragmatic": they are about the conditions in the discourse environment of the language learner, an environment that includes relations among competent speakers and between competent speakers and the novice, that must be satisfied if language entry is to occur. Nevertheless, there is a short step from these pragmatic considerations to epistemological issues.

38 Conceptual Structures

The structures hypothesized above as engaged in language learning look more like deductive structures than inductive ones. The judgment that if something is a dog then it is an animal is not probabilistic; it represents a semantic relation that is entrenched in the superordinate–subordinate hierarchies of languages. So one might wonder, once again, whether the abnormality of mutant predicates is that they do not fit into certain deductive structures implicit in languages and within which general terms must occupy nodes if they are to be candidates for inductive inferences. If so, then the account given above of the preconditions on normal general terms might be transformed into an analysis of entrenchment in terms of preconditions on projectible predicates (cf. Goodman, 1955). The fact that the above account of what is wrong with *grue* appeals to other predicates that happen already to exist in the language and to perceptual categories that are fixed by the practices of the language community now becomes highly relevant. Once we leave the domain of preconditions for the learnability of languages by humans, we may be tempted to consider whether those deductive structures that are apparently required for entrenchment of a predicate might be created by those who already have a language, and, if the answer is "yes", whether grue-type predicates could then become inductively respectable, despite their current abnormality.

I am inclined to think that the answer to this question is a guarded "yes"; an available example tempts one to consider this possibility. It is an example from rumor of future applications of new technology in fiber optics. What is being entertained, according to the rumor, is the production of home furnishings such as rugs whose visible color can be changed at will by the owner. If the ranges of color changes made possible by such a technology might be restricted to, say, changes from green to blue for one object and from red to yellow for another; and if the changes might be irreversible and might be programmed to take effect at a particular time, then the circumstances for entrenchment and projectibility of *timecolor*, *grue* and *rellow* will have been effected, it seems.[3] For these conditions to be fulfilled, however, a technology is required that will connect these predicates, via appropriate nodes, to superordinates, subordinates and, ultimately, to basic categories and their members.

39   Towards a Topology of Concepts

Independently of the considerations about language acquisition that have framed the above research, Peter Gärdenfors has offered a topological analysis of differences between the concepts *green* and *grue* in an effort to represent structurally the anomolous character of *grue* that makes it what he calls "unnatural" (Gärdenfors, 1990).[4] Although he construes his analysis as "non-linguistic", I think it is fair to say that this is meant in the sense of "non-sentential" or "non-truth-theoretic" rather than as denying the relevance of his analysis to our understanding of cognitive structures that may in fact be contingent upon human language. Indeed, one of the motivations of Gärdenfors's account is the construction of a topological theory of concepts that will provide solutions to problems in the semantics of natural language. Gärdenfors's topological account of the deviance of *grue* and my naturalistic one in terms of learnability theory appear to be complementary in many respects, although there are certain important divergences.

Gärdenfors's analysis of *grue* is presented as an application of his theory of conceptual spaces, a theory he develops in several papers and which is intended to provide non-sentential models for psychological structures of knowledge representation within Artificial Intelligence (AI). To understand the analysis of *grue* this theory provides, and also because the theory suggests possibilities for formal analyses of other cognitive properties and features this essay has introduced informally, I shall first attempt a general sketch of his central theory of conceptual spaces.[5]

The non-sentential representations provided by the theory are topological structures. Here are the fundamental concepts of the theory, described merely to suggest their intended representational use. A *conceptual space* or conceptual subspace consists of a class of *quality dimensions*. A *property* is defined as a *region of a conceptul space*. Each *point* in a region represents an object, or "possible individual", in virtue of representing a possible assignment of properties to an individual (Gärdenfors, 1990, p. 86).

A relevant example will help and will also bring us closer to the theory's account of *grue*. One conceptual subspace within the space of perception is the color space. The color space can be described in terms of the three (psychological) quality dimensions of hue, saturation, and brightness. Each of these dimensions can, in turn, be characterized and contrasted topologically. The dimension of hue, for example, differs topologically from that of brightness in that one hue may be opposite to another hue in the color circle, as is the case with complementary colors, whereas brightness is a quality dimension which is topologically linear and, so, does not manifest a relation of opposition.

According to Gärdenfors's analysis, *grue* and *green* differ significantly in their topological representations. First, he introduces the notion of a *natural property* as a region of a conceptual space that is *convex*. A convex region is one such that, for every pair of points in the region, any point that is *between* them is also in the region. The property *green* is a region of the color space that is convex, since, for any two (possible) objects whose color is green, any other object that lies between them in the color space will also be green. The timecolor *grue*, however, does not occupy a convex region, because there are pairs of objects that are grue but between which there are points that are not grue, that is, points representing green objects after the indexed time (Gärdenfors uses the year 2000 in his example) (Gärdenfors, 1990, p. 89). Gärdenfors conjectures that only convex properties are inductively projectible.

40   Conceptual Spaces and Cognitive Practices

Let me begin by reflecting on the relevance of the theory of conceptual spaces to the issues I have raised with some general remarks and then move on to compare Gärdenfors's account of *grue* with my own. Supposing that the general theory of conceptual spaces does accurately represent conceptual structures, the considerations raised in this essay suggest that not all cognitive structures available to the individual are conceptual. In particular, I have argued that pre-linguistic cognitive stuctures may be initially sensory structures and, subsequently, perceptual categories that are not yet conceptual. Any effort to construct realistic representations of cognitive structures should aim to represent differences among these types of structures as well as to model transformations of pre-conceptual structures into conceptual structures. Additionally, however, there is evidence of a non-personal level of conceptual and other cognitive structures embodied in the linguistic and behavioral practices of a linguistic community and these also need representation. Finally, it seems obvious that a topology of concepts alone will not do justice to the role of syntax, logical and linguistic, in the cognitive life of humans.

Here, now, are some of the convergences and divergences between the two accounts of what is wrong with *grue*. Where my account is continuous with developmental (cognitive) psychology, Gärdenfors has construed the problem in terms of knowledge representation within AI. Thus the level of abstraction of the two accounts might be expected to differ, although one should hope both for coherence between accounts at these two levels of abstraction and for theoretical challenges from either level to the other. Both can be found. One example of such interaction arises from the notion of conceptual spaces defined in terms of quality dimensions that Gärdenfors proposes. Gärdenfors describes quality dimensions, such as color, weight, and time, as "pre-linguistic" on the grounds that one can think about these qualities of objects "without presuming a language in which these thoughts can be expressed" (1990, p. 84). However, if the naturalistic account proposed herein is correct, this reason might better sustain the claim that such dimensions are non-linguistic or supra-linguistic than that they are pre-linguistic. Pre-linguistic perceptual categories may be related only tenuously to conceptual categories of weight, color, and time that emerge with superordination. Gärdenfors's main thesis, on the other hand, that the topological structures of the conceptual spaces of "unnatural" concepts are fundamentally different from those of "natural" (for humans) concepts suggests intriguing possibilities for a more rigorous representation of the semantic hierarchies that I have alleged are essentially engaged in human language learning than I have here attempted.

Two other comparisons can be mentioned here. First, if basic categories function as I have proposed, first as perceptual categories and then as transformed into conceptual categories, then the question can be asked how these two functions might be contrasted topologically; for although mere pattern recognition plays a role in the emergence of perceptual categories, perceptual categories seem to be both more than mere patterns recognized and less than conceptual categories.

Finally, while my account recognizes, with Gärdenfors, a certain human-relativity to our conceptualizing that accounts for the fact that some concepts are unnatural for us, I locate this relativity not in the bounded abstract structures of the concepts in isolation but in the location of *those* structures within other structures, including the richer but less tidy structures of practices. This contrast is what permits my account but not Gärdenfors's to envision the circumstances above in which *grue* might *become* natural, and thus projectible.

41   Meaning as Analogical

The foregoing proposals for a revised theory of language acquisition encourage a certain conception of the development of natural linguistic meaning for the individual. On this conception, linguistic meaning (intension/sense) has its psychological origination with the addition of predicates of the E-language (cf. Chomsky, 1986) to a primary store of perceptual categories on which early speech is based. These perceptual categories, in turn, emerge from the interaction of an individual's predispositions to make sensory groupings with a variety of manifestations of the community's entrenched categories. Both the sensory and the perceptual levels may tolerate idiosyncratic degrees of difference among individual users; certainly, greater degrees of difference are tolerable at the sensory level than at the level of perceptual categorization simply because it is at the latter level that a first degree of stability in usage across individuals within the language community is attempted. Indeed, at the sensory level, there may be vast individual differences in whatever psychological content might form some basis for the infant's verbalization – even though members of the adult community are wont to project their own rather uniform interpretations on the supposed content of the infants' vocalizations. All that is required for the infant to get set to proceed to the level of forming perceptual categories is that the extensions of their uses of words should intersect the extensions of uses of the community at large, presumably with some degree of coincidence that is greater than chance. It does not matter, then, in virtue of what features of those extensions the infant uses the same vocalizations; only the overt result and not the process need be the same across users.

It is interesting to note that Keil and Kelley (1987, p. 493) remark that Carey's earlier (1978) model of word meaning acquisition "suggested that, early in development, many word meanings are represented in terms of haphazard examples, which can be highly idiosyncratic;" and that Carey's research of that time had been influenced by Vygotsky.[6] However, they note this fact while setting about arguing that Vygotsky was mistaken in his conjecture that children undergo a global shift in word usage from "instance-based" to "principled". Their contention has been discussed above in chapter 3 (subsection 24.22) where an alternative interpretation of Vygotsky's claim is considered and endorsed, the alternative that is ultimately described as a shift from perceptual to conceptual categories, but categories that are not mediated by necessary and sufficient conditions for membership in them. Instead, a category is to be identified by its location in a network, where some terms in the network are also first associated with perceptual categories (Rosch's "basic categories").

Such stability in language use as there is, and as there must be if language is to function as it does in cognitively charged interpersonal exchange, can be attributed in the first place to the activity of conceptual categorizing. Not that the activity is in any clear way distinct from its results, the conceptual categories, in the normal course of interpersonal communication. The distinction between the activity and its results becomes apparent only in analyzing such phenomena as language acquisition, radical theory change and conceptual revolution. Although language acquisition has been our focus so far, when any of these three phenomena occurs, analogy rather than composition out of elements seems to be the uniformly relevant cognitive operation that marks their transitional phases. However, I am not concerned here to argue the general case but only that in the case of language acquisition, perceptions of similarity are all that are needed to start one towards the straight and narrow, *even where the similarity that one notices is not the similarity that another notices.*

On this account linguistic meaning for the individual arises, as many philosophers from Carnap through Goodman and Quine have remarked in different ways, through noticed similarity. It would be more accurate, however, to describe the relevant processes as processes of analogy rather than of similarity, since similarity is commonly understood as similarity with respect to particular properties or features whereas the relevant process in this case may be entirely non-specific with regard to properties or features, in addition to being idiosyncratic.[7]

The alternative to the Standard Theory suggested by the account of human cognitive development sketched so far replaces an atomistic account of linguistic meaning in the developing individual with an analogical one. There is some affinity here with Quine's notion of "innate similarity spaces", according to which the infant comes equipped with a means for judging, given three stimuli, A, B, and C, that A is closer to C than B is to C. The differences from Quine's account are, however, considerable. Quine (1960) has the prelinguistic infant equipped with propositional structures with which to conduct its commerce with the world; its first verbal forays are thus interpreted sententially. And, on Quine's account, when fluency is acquired, what come to be known are, centrally, concepts understood atomistically in terms of their (set) extensions in the world. Thus, Quine's account begins as strongly Realistic in the sense of presupposing a world of objects, properties, and relations about which language will be only a vehicle that enables the learner to converse and reason. A world of human-independent objects, properties and relations with which the learner must become acquainted in order to carry out these functions seems also presupposed. On these counts, Quine's semantics seems to be a referential semantics (section 9). Puzzlement sets in, however, when from such banal origins are derived the theses of the Indeterminacy of Translation and the Inscrutability of Reference (Quine, 1960 and 1969), for these seem to undercut presumptions of Scientific Realism in the theory as well as the privileged status accounted to first-order logic.

On Quine's account, human fallibility displays itself primarily when new evidence prompts or requires that a change be made in what is counted as true and secondarily in false or nonsensical beliefs about what objects there really are to be talked about. Human fallibility countenances change even in beliefs about logic, for the "laws of logic" may themselves be altered as a last resort if the evidence so demands. But although such laws are often

construed pragmatically by Quine – as rules of intellectual conduct – it is their semantics, their truth or falsehood, that is on the
line when their revision is contemplated. The present account
differs from Quine's mainly in assigning a much larger role in the
formation of cognitive practices to language learning, and a com-
paratively lesser role to "the objective pull". The elaboration of
this theme occupies the following section and beyond.

42 Discourse Genres

Throughout this essay, I have focused so exclusively on hypotheses concerning the character of the earliest development of discursive skills that I have virtually excluded consideration of the
topics that are most often the focus in philosophy of language, in
particular, the general theory of syntactic structure and its relations to logical structure. This one must do if one aims to abjure,
even programmatically, presumptions of innate mental syntax or
content.[8] Another reason for having avoided up to now discussion of children's syntax and of relations between logical syntax
and linguistic syntax is that current theories of both have often
seemed driven by a favored metaphysics and I have wanted to
avoid discussion that is purely at the level of metaphysical or
ontological disputation (cf. chapter 1, subsection 6.3). Having
come this far, however, the way is now open to address how the
categorial hypotheses above may be related to the complex structures of syntactic analysis – of logic and of language. To this end,
let me introduce a science-fiction example.

If we were to beep a complete grammar and lexicon of, say,
English to Martians and they were to come here producing strings
of sounds that were indistinguishable from English sentences, it
is most unlikely that they would be speaking English. The problems that would preclude this likelihood devolve largely around
two putative facts: first, that natural linguistic meaning and reference for humans is analogical rather than essential (as just
described). Entry into a human language requires membership
in a social institution within which some chains of perceived
similarities among stimuli are deemed sufficiently important to be

taken note of by entrenching them in named categories, by means of general terms. This enterprise presupposes the possibility of common awareness of noticed stimuli which the Martians cannot be presumed to share.

A second problem for the Martians is more obviously social-institutional. Discourses themselves – of whatever length – also come in different categories so that to construct, to understand or to enter into a discourse with others requires a mastery of certain skills in working with these meta-categories rather than merely propositional knowledge. Even if the Martians can recognize grammatical strings, they will have no mastery of our entrenched discourse practices. These discourse practices are central to human cognitive practices, the practices in which humans engage in order to better understand themselves and the world in which they find themselves.

Let us call these categories of discourse practices "discourse operators".[9] It is my contention that the understanding and construction of any discourse in a natural language requires its subsumption under at least one discourse operator; additionally, that this subsumption is itself part of a cognitive practice rather than, say, merely a calculation with uninterpreted symbols. As a practice, it requires skills at doing certain things over and above any propositional knowledge, even though these practices can themselves be propositionally described. The fact that different individuals have different discourse skills allows in principle for the unlikely possibility that some individuals might speak a language even though their discourse skills, and hence their cognitive capabilities, are limited to only one discourse operator. Certainly, some individuals prefer one discourse genre over other possible ones.[10]

The most widely understood type of discourse operator is perhaps the literary genre. Told that something is a novel, one is led to expect fiction, plot, character development, narrative, and the like; told that something is a classical tragedy, one is alerted to the unities of time, place and action, an heroic character in trying circumstances, a tragic flaw; the discourse operator *lyric poem* is associated with rhyme, tropes, images, and meter. But it is not familiar to think of genres as discourses "governed" by certain operations.

The notion of a sentence operator is more familiar. The sentence operation of negation, 'It is not the case that — ', operates on an assertion to turn it into a denial. A cluster of sentence operations can turn assertions into questions, for example, 'That is a book' into 'What is that?'. And there are sentence operators for modality, adjective derivation and so on. While it is most natural to think of sentence operators as operating syntactically on one sentence to turn it into another sentence (or sentence particle), discourse operators do not easily accommodate such a characterization. Discourse operators, instead, seem more felicitously characterized as rules, instructions, principles, or maxims for constructing and understanding a discourse. Rather than being purely syntactic, they normally have and depend upon pragmatic, syntactic, and semantic features.

That there are such cognitive meta-categories as discourse operators represent seems consequent upon this fact: the very same discourse which is, in fact, a novel (consider, for example, *The Name of the Rose*), and which is written and read as a novel, could, as far as anything internal to the discourse is concerned, be any number of other things: a biography, a police report, a history. But it is written, and read, as something quite different, a novel. What operator governs a discourse is, then, very important in determining its construction and its interpretation – as well as what dimensions of assessment are relevant to it. For example, it is not a criticism of a novel that its statements are not true of any real person. Discourse operators represent tacit knowledge of the members of the relevant linguistic community, knowledge of how to construct, intepret, and understand different discourses in accordance with their intended or other felicitous purposes. However, it need not be supposed that categories of discourse practices are universal across languages.

Just as literary genres are created and pass away – the classical tragedy or the epic poem, for example – discourse operators are etched not in stone but in the collective memories and practices of a linguistic community. Hence, the discourse operators that govern the *Tao Te Ching* and the *Chuang Tzu* may not be understood clearly by Westerners in general. Perhaps they are understood best only by members of the relevant practicing communities of Buddhists and Taoists. Numerous other examples lace the history of efforts to understand both alien and native tongues and texts. Discourse operators are socially contingent phenomena.

Suppose that one commands a range of discourse operators; how does one know which is the relevant one to use in understanding a particular discourse? Normally, by contextual clues – under what circumstances (including linguistic context; for example, what it is called) the discourse occurs. Given the multiplicity of possible language uses, we may hypothesize that it is essential to human language that there be discourse operators and that every discourse is governed by at least one such operator.

To illustrate the type of structure intended by the above very sketchy description, I turn now to a characterization of some salient features of the discourse operator *scientific report*, with the caveat that, as conceived here, such operators are historical occurrences that codify certain cognitive and other practices and which, along with those practices, are capable of change. We can distinguish, roughly, three types of rules or guiding principles, which can be understood as directions for constructing and understanding such a discourse: syntactic, semantic, and pragmatic ones. This typology is adopted here entirely for expository simplicity and is not meant as a recommended style of representing such practices. These "rules" are intended to be in no way surprising, of course, and each admits of justifiable exceptions and alternative statement:

Syntactic

1. Construct the discourse in accordance with the laws of classical logic (bivalence, excluded middle, non-contradiction, and so on).
2. Use declarative sentences in the indicative mood.

Semantic

3. Use words in accordance with the practices of the relevant scientific community.
4. Avoid tropes; at most, introduce only one.
5. Avoid ambiguity; use each categorematic term in one sense only, each individual name (if any; see 7 and 8) to refer to the same individual throughout.

6. Introduce only one discovery in one report.
7. Refer to idiosyncratic phenomena only by way of drawing a generalization, or illustrating exceptions to generalizations.

Pragmatic

8. Make no references to individuals except by way of citation.
9. Do not use indexical expressions (that is, do not use such expressions as 'this' or 'that' except anaphorically.)
10. Use referentially transparent constructions.

43   Non-Gricean Pragmatics

The notion of discourse operators sketched here is related to Paul Grice's characterization of conversations in his famous "Logic and Conversation" (Grice, 1975). Grice's essay was offered and has been widely accepted as vindicating the role of classical first-order logic as primary in human thought against challenges that the informal study of natural language practices had been seen as providing, particularly in the work of J. L. Austin and the late work of Wittgenstein in England at the mid-century.

Grice articulated general pragmatic conditions that apply to conversations in order to advance the view that conversational discourse does not conflict with the formal syntactic and semantic features of inference that are investigated in logic and formal semantics, features that have sometimes been proposed as characterizing an ideal language of science. Grice's conditions on conversational discourse incorporate knowledge of the world, such as the likely presuppositions of one's interlocutors. When these pragmatic conditions, together with the relevant world-knowledge, are taken into account, conversational discourse is seen by Grice to be compatible with the formal features of inference (and meaning) that are explicitly displayed by, for example, scientific discourse. The implications of Grice's pragmatics are that empirical studies of discourse do not reveal classical formal logic to be violated and that a thesis of its primacy in thought can be retained.

Apparent departures from the structures of classical deductive logic in discourse are to be accounted for by appealing to "pragmatic maxims" which, in effect, supply suppressed premises and other logical elements which reveal the apparent violations to be only surface perturbations of an underlying uniform logic.

The notion of a discourse operator is not incompatible with Grice's account but differs from it in several respects. First, it permits us to avoid the assumption that the formal features of some ideally conceived scientific discourse occupy a privileged position in understanding human natural language; scientific report discourse is seen as instantiating a linguistic discourse operator equally with conversational discourse regardless of its possible epistemic priority among human interests. Second, where Grice's account must explain such phenomena as metaphor, irony and, one may suppose, all other discourse operators as deviations from one or more conditions on "conversations" – and thus as twice removed from the presumed scientific discourse norm – the account proposed here would subsume such discourse modes on equal footing unless other considerations about the natural language should justify some ordering among discourse modes; irony, for example, seems constitutively a dependent operator while metaphor may not be. An advantage of such initial democracy among discourse modes is that it allows for two possibilities that otherwise seem recalcitrant: that meaning in natural languages is basically analogical, so that metaphor and other tropes are not to be accounted for naturalistically as deviations from a privileged, but elusive, "literal" sense; and that scientific discourse is a highly specialized development of natural language, permitted by it but not required by it.

It is time to recall that this essay was motivated as an effort to articulate a coherent account of the cognitive adaptive utility of human languages, one that would avoid metaphysical platforming as well as ascriptions of cognitive sophistication where there is no evidence for it. The final topics to be raised concern the bearing of these, tentative, conclusions about the nature of predication to other cognitive and epistemic concerns, in particular, to the substructural indeterminacy of predicates and the social contingency of beliefs.

44 Socially Contingent Phenomena

Several philosophers have argued that important features of language have an irreducible social component and so cannot be understood as issuing exclusively from processes or procedures within the individual speaker-hearer. Tyler Burge, in "Individualism and the Mental" (1979) and elsewhere, has argued that word meaning has an essentially social component; and Hilary Putnam, in "The Meaning of 'Meaning'" (1975) and other works, has proposed that there is a "division of linguistic labor", that is, that the reference or extension of a particular word, 'gold' for example, may not be determinable by any knowledge that the fluent speaker has but, instead, only by experts who have specialized non-linguistic or world knowledge. Burge and Putnam have thus called attention to semantic features of a language which do not supervene upon processes internal to the language user or the language learners, meaning and extension. The present essay has intended to add to this list of socially contingent linguistic phenomena certain structures that are fundamental to human cognitive enterprises.

When a phenomenon requires reference to interpersonal social relations for its understanding, I shall call the phenomenon a "socially contingent phenomenon". It is unproblematic that some things are socially contingent phenomena: they would not exist or would not be the kind of thing that they are but for the fact that there are certain types of interpersonal relations. Wars, universities, and marriages could not exist unless there were certain interpersonal relations. They are, we may say, "existentially" socially contingent. Other things, such as the artifacts of material culture – paintings, flags, churches – could not be what they are unless there were certain interpersonal relations. These we may call "essentially" social contingent phenomena. In the case of both types, the socially contingent items are what they are not by virtue of some uniquely determinate substructure, as gold, water, or a lemon are purported to be, but instead by virtue of the superstructures into which they enter, the relevant interpersonal relations. They are, we may say, substructurally indeterminate.

45   The Attitudes as Socially Contingent

The considerations made in this essay offer some persuasive reasons for thinking that the cognitive propositional attitudes, and in particular *believing that*, are socially contingent phenomena, at least essentially and, very likely, existentially. Independently of the considerations made in this essay, these seem language-dependent and, whatever our natural predilections towards acquiring a human language, we do not acquire one without relating interpersonally. The linguistic and hence social contingency of the cognitive attitudes, furthermore, would provide some basis for the desired account of the cognitive adaptive utility that human languages seem to provide (cf. section 5). How, exactly, does having beliefs depend upon interpersonal linguistic exchanges and what features of beliefs are derived from such exchanges?

There is general agreement among theorists that for a person to have a belief is, typically, for that person to predicate some property of a subject; that a belief, whatever else it may be, has the general structure: *that* is F (or, a is F, and so on). On their face, the propositional attitudes look discursive; they employ the distinction between subject and predicate which is paradigmatically found in declarative sentences of a language. Standard theories of language, mind, and logic may perform various operations by which objects for the propositional attitudes are distilled out of any linguistic substance which might contain them, but the considerations made here suggest that predication may be analyzed coherently as an acquired cognitive skill. In particular, they suggest that any psychological distinctions there may be between (thinking of) subjects and (thinking of) predicates, and between thinking of individuals or of properties are acquired by humans in the course of learning a language within the linguistic community. Indeed, they suggest that predication itself is a socially contingent phenomenon, and, along with it, all the propositional attitudes and any mental structures that are isomorphic with them.

This position, we have seen, does not require that we deny that humans or other animals have some "mental life" independently of learning an E-language, for of course there would be no acquiring an E-language unless there were directed attention, and directed attention must have some content. The problems – and confusions – arise when we attempt to *characterize* any non-socially contingent content of that attention. For what has emerged as a central possibility from the above is that all our conceptual categories – our predicates, our general terms – are, in some measure, socially contingent phenomena. But this is to say that all our concepts may be artifacts.[11] It does not, however, amount to saying that they are purely conventional, much less that they are arbitrary.

There is more than a suspicion that when theorists claim that humans have an "innate knowledge of truth", or that other animals and pre-linguistic infants "have beliefs", they actually mean to refer to the non-socially-contingent content of non-linguistically informed attention and awareness, and not to what I have here called "conceptual categories", nor, therefore to what I have called the cognitive skill of predication. A capacity for predication requires the ability to make multiple predications of differing orders of generality of the same subject. Hence, a natural test of predication would focus on the contrast between flexibility versus fixity of response to a stimulus under relevantly stable conditions (cf. Brandon, 1990, pp. 38–9).

46   Substructural Indeterminacy

The account of linguistic development that has been given must be regarded as a "middle-out" account, rather than either "top-down" or "bottom-up", since, on this account, predication is acquired as a cognitive location within a nested hierarchical ordering. It is this middle-out feature of the structures of predicate relations that allows that there may be predicates that are substructurally indeterminate. An individual can know that something is, for example, a physical object without knowing what determinate substructure, if any, that thing, or physical objects in general, have. But also, one can investigate to discover the determinate substructures of appropriate candidates, such as gold, water, or a lemon (or, for that matter, of inappropriate candidates, such as beliefs, or language, or mental content).

Alternatively, one can know that something is a university, a war, or a language without ever supposing that there is a determinate substructure essential to these things – or to their predicates. Substructural indeterminacy subtends our ability to talk about things that we don't know everything about as well as our efforts to know more; to discursively represent new information and to correct inadequate beliefs.

Substructural indeterminacy is not a univocal notion, however. It can be applied in one sense to the semantic content of a predicate, and in another sense to the items in the domain of a predicate – in either case, correctly or incorrectly.

Furthermore, the system itself which the language initiate enters may be characterized as substructurally indeterminate, since the nested hierarchies of predicates is. And this substructural indeterminacy of the system may be passed on to any products of the interaction of individual with system, in particular, to the discursive beliefs of the language user themselves. For, consider this: Does the child, prior to the achievement of superordination, who says 'A bird is a robin' believe that robins are the only birds? We might say "yes" on the grounds that the child applies both terms/words as if they named coextensive and so identical sets. But we might say "no" on the grounds that the child does not have predication, and so does not have the predicates 'is a bird' or 'is the only bird' or 'name coextensive sets.' But this phenomenon is not limited to the pre-superordination case. Hence, in describing a subject's belief content, we have the option of using our names and predicates for the objective phenomena or using the subject's. We choose one or the other depending largely on pragmatic considerations such as the task we are undertaking by means of our description and our estimate of our hearer's understanding and interests. Both discourse modes *correctly* describe the content of the subject's belief: such content is not uniquely determinate. If the content of a person's belief is equivalent to *its* location in a nested hierarchy of categories then that location may be variously described with equal accuracy.

A demand or expectation that meaning be definite and determinate reveals a mere metaphysical preference – from one side or the other of the Platonist/Physicalist divide. It is equally absurd to aim to purge our discourse of substructurally indeterminate predicates: If we suppose that one of the cognitive advantages by which language benefits humans is by expanding the range of possible interpersonal relations, thereby increasing benefits from cooperative behavior, then it is crucial to have such finer-grained assessments of others as our propositional attitudes provide.[12] It does not matter whether beliefs can be associated with neuronal or computational states of organisms, except to one who aspires to constrain their commerce with others to those domains.

I have intended herein to introduce certain lines of inquiry and to sketch a direction for investigation in which the questions raised at the beginning of this essay might be located, and the search for answers begun. While I am satisfied, for the moment, that this is the direction in which to go for an understanding of the relations between language and knowledge, I am also aware that the inventory of questions now exceeds the inventory of answers.

Notes

1 Note that I do not mean that 'grue' cannot be a color term because any particular thing that *is* grue undergoes a color change, for that is not true. I mean that the (presumed) color itself that grue would be if 'grue' were a color term would change in color so that any grue thing examined after the indexed time would be a different color (namely, blue) than those grue things examined before the indexed time, which would be green; hence the color grue would change in color. Colors do not do this; so 'grue' cannot be a color term.

2 In "Natural Kinds," Quine (1969) raises issues related to these, first considering the notions of kind and of similarity to be interdefinable and ideally eliminated by an advanced science. Reflecting further on the "sense of comparative similarity" posited as innate in *Word and Object* (1960) he considers, and finds wanting, the explanatory usefulness of the notion that "*the kind with paradigm a and foil b* is the set of all the things to which a is more similar than a is to b" 1969, pp. 119–20. From the present perspective, a naive ontological realism is built into an approach such as this one that assumes our general terms to map simply into ontological kinds without acknowledging that the terms are relative to an adventitious language. Such a realism may, however, be felicitous or even necessary to our scientific practices.

3   The predicates in the current example differ from Goodman's by not being in general indexed to a specific time but the example illustrates how the superordinate *timecolor* might become entrenched and projectible – via the imagined technology. Once we have this predicate entrenched, we can then conceive of different families of timecolors, $grue_1$ indexed to the year 2000, $grue_2$ indexed to the year 2004, and so forth.

4   Gärdenfors' account and the present proposal were developed entirely independently of one another; in the brief description of his analysis that follows, I hope my misunderstandings are minimal.

5   The general account I sketch is drawn from Gärdenfors (1990), although he has developed this account in several other places.

6   Recall that it was argued (subsection 24.22) that Keil and Kelley's claim to have produced counterevidence to Vygotsky's model is based upon an interpretation of his model that is not optimal. They assume that the shift to what Vygotsky calls "principled" conceptual thinking is, paradigmatically, a shift from instance-based thinking to thinking that is based on defining features (that is, necessary and sufficient conditions). Better in accord with Vygotsky's account is the hypothesis that early, instance-based thinking represents a range from highly idiosyncratic sensory uptake to the formation of perceptual categories. The shift to "principled" conceptual thinking may be, first, the result merely of the formation of perceptual categories, prior to the formation of *any* conceptual categories. At the hypothesized stage of the formation of perceptual categories, prior to conceptualization, uniformities of usage develop. Furthermore, it would seem that such perceptual categories are in no way based upon defining features where these are understood as necessary and sufficient conditions.

7   Wittgenstein's proposal that, for some words, their meaning be reconstrued as family resemblance is relevant to this proposed shift from a focus on similarity in respect of certain features or properties to a focus on non-specific analogy. See also Ross's *Portraying Analogy* (1981) and Kittay's *Metaphor: Its Cognitive Force and Linguistic Structure* (1987).

8   The emphasis here is on "presumptions", for certainly humans come into the world with some normal species equipment – even though this equipment may be *less* than the endowments of members of other species.

9   I borrow the expression "discourse operator" from Paul Ziff; both it and the idea that scientific reports constitute a special discourse domain derive from the Discourse Analysis Project at the University of Pennsylvania that was directed by Zellig Harris and Henry

Hiż. These predecessors are in no way responsible for the particular uses developed here. On the other hand, these uses are intended to capture some of the features of Wittgenstein's notion of language games (1953).

10 Large segments of intellectual history lend themselves to analysis in terms of the political power of one discourse genre over others. The genres of religious and philosophical discourses no less than ideological and political genres have been accorded positions of favor within social and political power structures. The discourse of Scientific Realism is only one such genre among many, albeit a favored one in this century. (I beg the reader not to take this comment as itself the endorsement of some other genre – relativism, Marxism, or skepticism, for example.)

11 I should want to insist upon a difference between saying that all our conceptual categories are artifacts and theses of "meaning holism", but must leave this distinction for another time.

12 Pinker and Bloom (1990), fair proponents of the Standard Theory, have argued that the benefits to social interaction provided by language contribute to its adaptive advantage for evolutionary selection. Their focus, it should be noted, is principally on evolutionary advantages of the *syntactic* complexities of human languages.

References

Alston, William 1964: *Philosophy of Language*. Englewood Cliffs, NJ: Prentice-Hall.

Anglin, Jeremy 1970: *The Growth of Word Meaning*. Cambridge, MA: MIT Press.

Anglin, Jeremy 1977: *Word, Object and Conceptual Development*. New York: W. W. Norton.

Barcan Marcus, Ruth 1990: "Some revisionary proposals about belief and believing." *Philosophy and Phenomenological Research*, L Supplement, 133–53.

Barwise, Jon 1989: *The Situation in Logic*. Stanford, CA: Center for the Study of Language and Information.

Barwise, Jon, and Perry, John 1983: *Situations and Attitudes*. Cambridge, MA, and London: MIT Press.

Bealer, George 1982: *Quality and Concept*. Oxford: Clarendon Press.

Bealer, George, and Mönnich, Uwe 1989: "Property Theories." In D. Gabbay and F. Guenther (eds), *Handbook of Philosophical Logic*, Dordrecht, Boston, MA: D. Reidel, vol. 4, 133–251.

Bennett, Jonathan 1976: *Linguistic Behavior*. Cambridge: Cambridge University Press.

Berlinski, David 1976: *On Systems Analysis*. Cambridge, MA: MIT Press.

Blackman, Derek E. 1991: "B. F. Skinner and G. H. Mead: On biological science and social science." *Journal of the Experimental Analysis of Behavior*, 55, 251–65.

Block, Ned 1980: "Introduction: What is functionalism?" In *Readings in Philosophy of Psychology*, Cambridge, MA: Harvard University Press, vol. 1.

Brandon, Robert N. 1985: "Phenotypic plasticity, cultural transmission, and human sociobiology." In James H. Fetzer (ed.), *Sociobiology and Epistemology*, Dordrecht, Boston, MA, Lancaster: D. Reidel.

Brandon, Robert N. 1990: *Adaptation and Environment*. Princeton, NJ: Princeton University Press.

Brown, Roger 1958: *Words and Things*. New York and London: The Free Press.

Brown, Roger 1973: *A First Language: The early stages*. Cambridge, MA: Harvard University Press.

Brown, Roger 1978: "A new paradigm of reference." In G. Miller and E. Lenneberg (eds), *Psychology and Biology of Language and Thought*, New York: Academic Press.

Burge, Tyler 1979: "Individualism and the mental." In *Midwest Studies in Philosophy*, vol. IV, ed. P. A. French, T. E. Uehling, and H. K. Wettstein, Minneapolis: University of Minnesota Press.

Burge, Tyler 1986: "Individualism and psychology." *Philosophical Review*, 95, 3–45.

Carey, Susan 1978: "The child as word learner." In M. Halle, J. Bresnan and G. Miller (eds), *Linguistic Theory and Psychological Reality*, Cambridge, MA: MIT Press/Bradford Press.

Carey, Susan 1985: *Conceptual Change in Childhood*. Cambridge, MA: MIT Press.

Carnap, Rudolf 1928: *Der logische Aufbau der Welt*. Berlin: Weltkreis Verlag.

Carnap, Rudolf 1947: *Meaning and Necessity*. Chicago: University of Chicago Press.

Cherry, Colin 1957: *On Human Communication*. Cambridge, MA: Technology Press of MIT.

Chomsky, Noam 1965: *Aspects of the Theory of Syntax*. Cambridge, MA: MIT Press.

Chomsky, Noam 1986: *Knowledge of Language*. New York: Praeger.

Clark, E. V. 1987: "The principle of contrast." In B. MacWhinney (ed.), *The 20th Annual Carnegie Symposium on Cognition*, Hillsdale, NJ: Lawrence Erlbaum Associates.

Cocchiarella, Nino B. 1986: *Logical Investigations of Predication Theory and the Problem of Universals*, vol. 2 of *Indices*. Naples: Bibliopolis Press.

Davidson, Donald 1967: "Truth and Meaning." *Synthese*, 17, 304–23.

Davies, Martin 1991: "Individualism and perceptual content." *Mind*, 100, 461–84.

Dowty, David R., Wall, R. E. and Peters, S. 1981: *Introduction to Montague Semantics. Synthese Language Library*. Dordrecht, Boston, MA, London: D. Reidel.

Dretske, Fred 1969: *Seeing and Knowing*. London: Routledge & Kegan Paul.

Dretske, Fred 1981: *Knowledge and the Flow of Information*. Oxford: Basil Blackwell.

Dummett, Michael 1983: "Language and truth." In Roy Harris (ed.), *Approaches to Language*, Oxford: Pergamon Press.

Evans, Gareth 1982: *The Varieties of Reference*, ed. John McDowell. Oxford: Clarendon Press.

Fodor, Jerry 1975: *The Language of Thought*. New York: Crowell.

Fodor, Jerry A. 1981: *Representations*. Cambridge, MA: MIT Press.

Fodor, Jerry A. 1983: *The Modularity of Mind*. Cambridge, MA, and London: MIT Press.

Fodor, Jerry 1987: *Psychosemantics*. Cambridge, MA, and London: MIT Press.

Gärdenfors, Peter 1990: "Induction, conceptual spaces and AI." *Philosophy of Science*, 57, 78–95.

Gillett, G. R. 1987: "The generality constraint and conscious thought." *Analysis*, 47, 20–5.

Goodman, Nelson 1951: *The Structure of Appearance*. Cambridge, MA: Harvard University Press.

Goodman, Nelson. 1955: *Fact, Fiction, and Forecast*. Cambridge, MA: Harvard University Press.

Gopnik, Alison and Wellman, Henry M. 1992. "Why the child's theory of mind really *is* a theory." *Mind and Language*, 7, 145–71.

Grice, H. P. 1975: "Logic and conversation." In Peter Cole and Jerry L. Morgan (eds), *Syntax and Semantics*, New York: Academic Press. Reprinted in *Studies in the Way of Words*, Cambridge, MA, and London: Harvard University Press, 1989.

Hacking, Ian 1975: *Why Does Language Matter to Philosophy?* Cambridge: Cambridge University Press.

Hanfmann, E. and Kasanin, J. 1942: *Conceptual Thinking in Schizophrenia*. New York: Nervous Mental Disease Monographs.

Hare, R. M. 1952: *The Language of Morals*. London: Oxford University Press.

Harnad, Stevan 1987a: "Category induction and representation." In Stevan Harnad (ed.), *Categorical Perception*, Cambridge: Cambridge University Press.

Harnad, Stevan 1987b: "Uncomplemented categories; or, What is it like to be a bachelor?" Presidential Address to the 13th Annual Meeting of the Society for Philosophy and Psychology, University of California San Diego.

Harnad, Stevan (ed). 1987c: *Categorical Perception*. Cambridge: Cambridge University Press.

Hart, John Jr and Gordon, Barry 1992: "Neural subsystems for object knowledge." *Nature*, 359, 60–4.

Hartnett, William E. 1974: *Foundations of Coding Theory*. Dordrecht, Boston, MA: D. Reidel.

Hockett, Charles Francis 1958: *A Course in Modern Linguistics*. New York: Macmillan.

Horgan, Terence 1987: "Supervenient qualia." *Philosophical Review*, XCVI 491–520.

Huttenlocher, J. 1974: "The origins of language comprehension." In R. L. Solso (ed.), *Theories of Cognitive Psychology*, Hillsdale, NJ: Erlbaum.

Jakobson, Roman 1961: *Main Trends in the Science of Language*. London: George Allen & Unwin.

Johnson-Laird, P. N. 1983: *Mental Models*. Cambridge: Cambridge University Press.

Katz, J. J. and Fodor, J. A. 1964: "The structure of a semantic theory." *Language*, 39, 170–210.

Keil, Frank 1979: *Semantic and Conceptual Development*. Cambridge, MA: Harvard University Press.

Keil, Frank C. and Kelley, Michael H. 1987: "Developmental changes in category structure." In Stevan Harnad (ed.), *Categorical Perception*, Cambridge: Cambridge University Press.

Kim, Jaegwon 1978: "Supervenience and nomological incommensurables." *American Philosophical Quarterly*, 15, 149–156.

Kim, Jaegwon 1984: "Concepts of supervenience." *Philosophy and Phenomenological Research*, 65, 257–70.

Kittay, Eva Feder 1987: *Metaphor: its cognitive force and linguistic structure*. Oxford: Clarendon Press.

Kripke, Saul 1959: "A completeness theorem in modal logic." *Journal of Symbolic Logic*, 24, 1–14.

Kripke, Saul 1963: "Semantical considerations on modal logic." *Acta Philosophica Fennica*, 16, 83–94.

Lewis, David K. 1969: *Convention: a philosophical study*. Cambridge, MA: Harvard University Press.

Li, Charles N. and Thompson, Sandra A. 1978: "Subject and topic: a new typology of language." In Charles N. Li (ed.), *Subject and Topic*, Stanford, CA: Academic Press.

Locke, John 1706: *An Essay Concerning Human Understanding*, 5th edn. London.

Lycan, William 1984: *Logical Form in Natural Language*. Cambridge, MA: MIT Press.

Macnamara, John 1982: *Names for Things*. Cambridge, MA, and London: MIT Press.

Macnamara, John 1986: *A Border Dispute*. Cambridge, MA, and London: MIT Press.

Markman, Ellen M. 1989: *Categorization and Naming in Children*. Cambridge, MA, and London: MIT Press.

Markman, Ellen M. and Wachtel, Gwyn F. 1988: "Children's use of mutual exclusivity to constrain the meanings of words." *Cognitive Psychology*, 20, 121–57.

McGinn, Colin 1984: *Wittgenstein on Meaning*. Oxford: Basil Blackwell.

McGinn, Colin 1989: *Mental Content*. Oxford: Basil Blackwell.

Mead, George Herbert 1934: *Mind, Self and Society*, ed. Charles W. Morris. Chicago and London: University of Chicago Press.

Mead, George Herbert 1981: "The psychology of punitive justice." In Andrew J. Rech (ed.), *Selected Writings*, Chicago and London: University of Chicago Press.

Mill, John Stuart 1872: *System of Logic*, 8th edn. London.

Miller, George 1969: "The magical number seven, plus or minus two." In *The Psychology of Communication*. Baltimore, MD: Penguin Books.

Miller, G. A. and Johnson-Laird, P. N. 1976: *Language and Perception*. Cambridge, MA: Harvard University Press.

Miller, G. and Lenneberg, Elizabeth (eds) 1978: *Psychology and Biology of Language and Thought*. New York: Academic Press.

Millikan, Ruth Garrett 1984: *Language, Thought, and Other Biological Categories: new foundations for realism*. Cambridge, MA, and London: MIT Press.

Montague, Richard 1974: "English as a formal language." In R. H. Thompson (ed.), *Formal Philosophy: selected papers of Richard Montague*, New Haven, Conn: Yale University Press.

Nolan, Rita 1969: "Truth and sentences." *Mind*, 78, 501–11.

Nolan, Rita 1970: *Foundations for an Adequate Criterion of Paraphrase. Janua Linguarum no. 84*. The Hague: Mouton.

Palmer, Stephen E. 1978: "Fundamental aspects of cognitive representation." In E. Rosch and B. B. Lloyd (eds), *Cognition and Categorization*, Hillsdale, NJ: Lawrence Erlbaum, 259–303.

Pinker, S. and Bloom, P. 1990: "Natural language and natural selection." *Behavioral and Brain Sciences*, 13, 707–84.

Putnam, Hilary 1975: "The meaning of 'meaning'." In Keith Gunderson (ed.), *Language, Mind and Knowledge*, Minneapolis: University of Minnesota Press.

Putnam, Hilary 1981: *Reason, Truth and History.* Cambridge: Cambridge University Press.

Pylyshyn, Zenon 1984: *Computation and Cognition.* Cambridge, MA: MIT Press.

Quine, W. V. 1960: *Word and Object.* Cambridge, MA: MIT Press.

Quine, W. V. 1969: "Natural kinds." In *Ontological Relativity.* New York and London: Columbia University Press.

Quine, W. V. 1974: *Roots of Reference.* La Salle, Ill.: Open Court.

Ramsey, F. P. 1925: "Universals." Reprinted in D. H. Mellor (ed.), *Foundations: essays in philosophy, logic, mathematics and economics*, London and Henley: Routledge & Kegan Paul, 1978.

Rech, Andrew J. (ed.) 1981: *Selected Writings of George Herbert Mead.* Chicago and London: University of Chicago Press.

Rorty, Richard 1979: *Philosophy and the Mirror of Nature.* Princeton, NJ: Princeton University Press.

Rosch, E. 1978: "Principles of categorization." In E. Rosch and B. B. Lloyd (eds), *Cognition and Categorization*, Hillsdale, NJ: Erlbaum.

Rosch, E., Mervis, C. B., Gray, W. D., Johnson, D. M. and Boyes-Braem, P. 1976: "Basic objects in natural categories." *Cognitive Psychology*, 8, 382–439.

Ross, J. F. 1981: *Portraying Analogy.* Cambridge: Cambridge University Press.

Russell, Bertrand 1956: "The philosophy of logical atomism." In Robert C. Marsh (ed.), *Logic and Knowledge*, London: Allen & Unwin.

Ryle, Gilbert 1971: *Collected Papers.* New York: Barnes & Noble.

Schwyzer, Hubert 1990: *The Unity of Understanding: a study in Kantian problems.* Don Mills, ON, and New York: Oxford University Press.

Searle, John R. 1969: *Speech Acts.* Cambridge: Cambridge University Press.

Shannon, Claude and Weaver, Warren 1964: *The Mathematical Theory of Communication.* Urbana: University of Illinois Press.

Sibley, Frank 1959: "Aesthetic concepts." *Philosophical Review*, 68, 421–50.

Smillie, David 1985: "Sociobiology and human culture." In James H. Fetzer (ed.), *Sociobiology and Epistemology*, Dordrecht, Boston, MA, Lancaster: D. Reidel.

Stemmer, Nathan 1989: "The acquisition of the ostensive lexicon: the superiority of empiricist over cognitive theories". *Behaviorism*, 17, 41–61.

Stich, Stephen P. 1983: *From Folk Psychology to Cognitive Science.* Cambridge, MA, and London: MIT Press.

Strawson, P. F. 1959: *Individuals.* London: Methuen.

Strawson, P. F. 1971: "The asymmetry of subjects and predicates." In *Logico-linguistic Papers*, London and New York: Methuen.

Strawson, P. F. 1974: *Subject and Predicate in Logic and Grammar*. London: Methuen.

Tarski, A. 1944: "The semantic conception of truth." *Philosophy and Phenomenological Research*, 4, 341–75.

Tarski, A. 1956: "The concept of truth in formalized languages." In *Logic, Semantics, Metamathematics*, Oxford: Clarendon Press.

Tunmer, W. E. and Grieve, R. 1984: "Syntactic awareness in children." In W. E. Tunmer, C. Pratt and M. L. Herriman (eds), *Metalinguistic Awareness in Children*, Berlin: Springer-Verlag.

Von Schilcher, Florian and Tennant, Neil 1984: *Philosophy, Evolution and Human Nature*. London: Routledge & Kegan Paul.

Vygotsky, L. S. 1962: *Thought and Language*, tr. E. Hanfmann and G. Vakar. Cambridge, MA: MIT Press.

Vygotsky, L. S. 1978: *Mind in Society*, ed. M. Cole et al. London and Cambridge, MA: Harvard University Press.

Vygotsky, L.S. 1986: *Thought and Language*, tr. and ed. A. Kozulin. Cambridge, MA: MIT Press.

Wittgenstein, Ludwig 1953: *Philosophical Investigations*. New York: Macmillan.

Wittgenstein, Ludwig 1922: *Tractatus Logico-philosophicus*. London: Routledge & Kegan Paul.

Ziff, Paul 1960: *Semantic Analysis*. Ithaca, NY: Cornell University Press.

Index